Bible Stories For Kids

A Collection Of Captivating Religious Tales for Children to Teach Christian Moral Values, Jesus's Miracles, and Faith to Grow in God's Name.

Ella Swan

Contents

The Mysterious Tree

C lose your eyes and take a journey to a world where the sun stretches its rays over the cottony clouds during the day and the stars glitter in the darkness of the night like a billion silver earrings hanging from a big, black blanket.

The waves in the ocean are whispering. The wind sings as it makes the leaves of the trees dance. Can you hear them?

Now, imagine the rabbits with their floppy, furry ears racing across the meadow against the long-legged kangaroos. Picture penguins skating across slippery ice and ostriches stretching their necks while sitting on a bed of hot sand. Imagine a whale longer than three buses creating a big splash or a stick insect no bigger than your thumb trying to be, well, a stick.

This is the world God created a long, long time ago. A beautiful and peaceful world. A colorful world. A perfect world.

Even God was very happy with what He had made, but He also could not help but feel that there was something missing.

"What else can I add?" God wondered. "A unicorn? A flower that can sing? A sea of pure chocolate?"

He touched His fingertips together and stroked His chin as He thought, and soon, the idea came to Him.

"I know just what this beautiful world needs!" He exclaimed.

God gathered some dust in his hands, spat on it to make it into clay and then started making shapes, putting them together to make something with a head, two arms and two legs - a man! Then he poked two holes in the man's head and blew into it.

As he took his first breath, the clay man turned into a real man. He opened his eyes, stood on his feet, and looked at his hands. He was alive!

God was happy with his latest creation. Now, He just had to think of where to put the man.

First, God put the man inside a cave, but the man did not like the cave.

"It is too cold and too dark," he said.

Next, God put the man underwater, building a house with walls of coral and a seaweed roof, but the man almost drowned.

God then tried putting the man on an island in the middle of the sea, but it was too hot, and he did not like the sand because it tickled his feet.

"Where shall I put him then?" God wondered, trying to think of a place that was peaceful and beautiful and with plenty of food. Then He thought of the answer. "I shall build him a garden!"

This garden was like a work of art. It had red, purple, and orange flowers - any color you can think of - and plenty of trees with all kinds of delicious fruit for the man to eat - big, small, sour, sweet. It even had rivers running through it and plenty of gold and precious stones.

The man took one look at the garden, and he immediately felt at home.

"You can take whatever you need," God told him. "And eat any fruit from any tree except for that big tree."

God pointed to the tree with the thick trunk and the long branches that stood all by itself in the middle of the garden.

The man looked at it and felt puzzled. "It looks just like any other tree to me," he thought.

"And yet if you eat the fruit of that tree, your life will end," God warned him. "So make sure you stay away from it."

The man nodded. He was curious, of course, but there were plenty of other trees anyway.

Sometimes, he ate watermelons in the morning, tomatoes and lettuce for lunch, and grapes for dinner.

He ate, and he took walks among the flowers, and he pulled out the weeds. Sometimes, he would swim in the river, too. Then at night, he would sleep under the stars. The grass was his bed and leaves were his blanket.

It was a simple and peaceful life, but after some time, the man got bored. He would yawn and he would sigh. He would pull his ears and tap his feet on the ground.

God saw this and thought, "Maybe I should put some animals in the garden for the man to play with."

God put animals in the garden and told the man to give each of them a name.

"But I don't even have my own name," the man said.

"Hmm." God tried to think of a good name for the man. Then he grinned. "I shall call you 'Adam'. This will be your name from now on."

Adam liked his name, and he had fun giving the animals their names. He named a porcupine 'Pointy' and an armadillo 'Curly'. He also played games with the animals like hide-and-seek with the chameleon and hopscotch with the kangaroo.

It was hard taking care of the animals, though, like trimming the claws of the eagle and combing the hair of the yak. It was hard remembering all their names, too.

"I wish I had someone to help me," Adam said.

God heard Adam's prayer, and He decided to grant his wish.

One night, while Adam was dreaming of having a banana eating contest with a monkey, God reached inside his chest and took one of his ribs. Out of this rib God made a whole new person - a woman.

When Adam woke up, he saw the woman, and his eyes grew wide.

"She looks just like me!" he said. "But with such beautiful hair and soft skin."

"I made her from your bones," God told Adam. "So from now on, she will be yours. She will be your helper, your wife, and your friend."

"I will take good care of her," Adam promised. "But first, I must give her a name."

He stopped to think then turned to the woman. "I've given so many names and forgotten some so I'll just give you one that's easy to remember," he said. "Is it okay if I call you 'Eve'?"

The woman smiled. "Of course."

Adam took Eve's hand. "Eve, would you like to live in this garden with me?"

"I would love to," Eve said.

Suddenly, her stomach grumbled.

Adam laughed. "Don't worry. We have plenty of fruits to eat, except the one of the mysterious tree in the middle of the garden. We must not even touch its fruit or our lives will be in danger."

"Okay," Eve said. "I will only eat whatever you eat."

Adam and Eve stayed away from the mysterious tree. However, they were not the only ones who knew about the tree. The snake did, too, and it liked to cause trouble. One day, when Eve was alone, it wrapped itself around her leg and started hissing.

"Did God really say that you cannot eat the fruit of the tree in the middle of the garden?"

"Yes," Eve replied. "That is what Adam told me."

"And did he say why?"

Eve shook her head. "Only that I will be in danger if I even touch that fruit."

"But why?" the snake asked.

Eve shrugged. "Adam does not know why. God did not tell him."

The snake laughed, and Eve frowned.

"What is so funny?" she asked.

"You," the snake answered and laughed again. "You really believe a fruit can be so dangerous? God just wants to have the fruits of that tree all to himself because they are the best. If you eat them, you will start thinking like God."

Eve could not stop thinking about the snake's words. They slithered inside her head and hissed in her ear.

One day, she went to the middle of the garden. She was just going to take a peek at the mysterious tree, but as soon as she saw it, she became even more curious. What was so scary about this tree?

It did not have glowing eyes on its trunk or slime hanging from its branches. In fact, it looked just like any other tree, and its fruits looked so delicious that Eve's mouth started to water.

"I'm sure its fruits taste amazing," Eve thought.

She just had to taste one, so she reached out, and closing her eyes and holding her breath, touched one of the fruits.

Nothing happened.

Eve opened her eyes. She was fine just like the snake said, so maybe it was also telling the truth when it said eating the fruits of this tree would make her wise like God.

She grabbed the fruit and took a bite, then she picked more fruits and brought them back to Adam.

"I found the tastiest fruit in the garden," she said to him. "Try them and see for yourself."

Adam trusted Eve so he took a bite, and another, and another. The fruit was so delicious he could not stop eating.

They ate and ate, and when they had finished, they were fine, except for one thing that they had realized.

"Oh no!" Eve cried, covering herself. "Why am I not wearing any clothes? Surely, I have to wear something."

Adam agreed. "Maybe we can make some clothes out of leaves," he said.

Later, God came to visit the garden.

"Adam! Eve!" He called. "Where are you?"

Adam and Eve did not come out at first, afraid that God would not like their clothes. Sure enough, when God found them, He did not, not because they were made of leaves, but because He knew there was only one reason why Adam and Eve felt the need to wear them.

"You ate the fruit of the tree in the middle of the garden, didn't you?" He asked Adam.

Adam looked at Eve. "Do you mean the tasty fruit you gave me was from the tree in the middle of the garden?"

Eve nodded. "But I only went to the mysterious tree because the snake told me to. I was only curious. I did not mean to do anything wrong."

God looked at the snake. "Because of what you have done, from now on, you will crawl on the ground." Then He turned to Adam and Eve. "As for you both, you must leave this garden at once, never to return.

"But where will we sleep?" Adam asked. "What will we eat?"

"You will build your own house and look for your own food," God answered. "You will work everyday and when your lives are over, you will return to dust."

Adam and Eve were sad to hear this, but there was nothing they could do. They left the garden with its colorful flowers, exciting animals, and the mysterious tree.

Escape From The Wicked City

There are many nations in the world today, but did you know that one man was once called the father of them all? A long time ago, God chose a man named Abram and gave him a new name - Abraham, meaning 'Father of Nations', promising him that he would have more descendants than anyone could count.

In the beginning, he did not even have his own home, though. He traveled from place to place, living in tents with his wife, Sarah, and their servants. He also did not have any children of his own.

One day, when he was already almost a hundred years old, he saw three strangers outside his tent. As soon as he saw them, he knew they were messengers of God, so he ran to greet them.

"Please make yourself at home," Abraham told them. "Sit under the tree outside my tent, and I will bring you food and water."

The messengers sat under the tree, and Abraham gave them water. Then he ran inside his tent where Sarah was.

"Quick!" he told her. "I need enough bread for three people."

Sarah was surprised to know they had guests, but she nodded. "I will get it ready right away."

Then Abraham went to one of his servants, ordering him to prepare some meat.

"I have important guests," he said. "Let us serve them one of our best young cows."

When the food was ready, Abraham brought it to his guests. "Please eat as much as you like," he told them.

The first messenger took a bite and nodded. "This is good food."

Abraham smiled. "I'm glad you like it. My wife, Sarah, prepared this dish."

"Where is your wife?" the second messenger asked.

"Inside the tent," Abraham answered. "Is there something you want to tell her?"

"Just that she will have a son soon," the third messenger answered.

Abraham could not believe his ears. He had hoped that when God called him the 'Father of Nations' that he would finally have a son, but he was still surprised and thrilled.

Sarah had heard it, too, and she did not believe it, laughing.

"I am ninety years old now," she said to herself. "How am I supposed to have a child?"

The messengers heard her laugh, and they told Abraham, "Nothing is too difficult for God. Sarah will have a son. You will finally have a child."

Sarah stopped laughing, knowing she was wrong. So what if she was old? God was all-powerful. Instead of complaining, she should just be thankful. After all, her greatest wish was about to come true. She could not wait to hold her son in her arms.

After eating, the messengers left. Abraham decided to go walk with them for a while.

"Where are you going next?" he asked them.

"Sodom," the first messenger answered.

"I see." Abraham touched his beard. "That is where my nephew, Lot, lives with his family. He is a good man who also believes in God."

The three messengers suddenly stopped walking, their foreheads wrinkled.

"What's wrong?" Abraham asked them.

For a moment more, the messengers did not say a word, then the first one sighed and looked at Abraham.

"God has something to tell you," he said. "Something you might not like."

Abraham was even more eager to hear it now, his eyebrows like arches above his eyes. "What is it?"

"The cities of Sodom and Gomorrah have become wicked," the third messenger explained. "They have turned away from God and from good, so God is sending us there. If it is true that there is no hope for those cities, then God will destroy them."

"Destroy them?" Abraham's eyes grew wide with fear.

"Yes." The first messenger nodded. "So we must be on our way."

The messengers continued walking, leaving Abraham alone. Abraham just stood there, too shocked to move.

Was Sodom and Gomorrah really going to be destroyed? What about the people there? What about Lot and his family?

Abraham knelt down and prayed. "Dear God, please have mercy. I know there are wicked people in Sodom and Gomorrah, but there are also good people. Is it right for them to be punished, too? Please, dear God, if you find even fifty good people there, do not destroy those cities."

"Very well," God said. "Because you asked out of the goodness of your heart, if I find fifty good people in Sodom and Gomorrah, those cities will be saved."

"Thank you," Abraham said, but he was still worried, so he continued praying. "Dear God, I know I am only your servant, but please, may I ask this: If there are forty-five good people, not fifty, will you still show mercy?"

"Very well," God answered. "If I find forty-five good people, Sodom and Gomorrah will not be destroyed."

"What about if there are only forty?" Abraham dared to ask.

"If I find forty good people, Sodom and Gomorrah will not be destroyed," God said.

Abraham continued. "Dear God, please do not be angry with me, but please, if there are even twenty good people, spare the cities of Sodom and Gomorrah."

"Alright," God agreed. "I am a just and merciful God, so I will not destroy Sodom and Gomorrah for the sake of twenty good people."

Abraham felt touched by God's mercy, but he decided to ask one more time. "Dear God, I know I may be asking too much. I promise this is the last time I will try to change your mind. If you find even ten good people in Sodom and Gomorrah, please do not destroy those cities."

God paused, then said. "I will not punish Sodom and Gomorrah if I find even ten good people there."

"Thank you," Abraham said.

Then God left.

Abraham let out a breath of relief, but he was still worried. He could only hope that there would be at least ten good people in Sodom and Gomorrah.

In the evening, God's messengers arrived in Sodom. Like Abraham, Lot recognized them as soon as he saw them, and he ran to pay them his respects.

"Please stay at my house tonight," Lot invited them. "I will give you water to wash, food to eat, and warm beds to sleep in so you may rest."

But the first messenger shook his head. "We are going around the city tonight. We have a job to do."

Still, Lot insisted. "It is already late and surely, you must be tired after walking so far. Please rest at my house. I would be honored to have you as my guests."

The messengers looked at each other. "Very well," they said. "We will accept your invitation."

They followed Lot to his house.

Little did they know that someone was spying on them. By nightfall, a large group of people had gathered around Lot's house.

"We've heard you have guests, Lot!" they shouted. "Why don't you bring them out so we can meet them and be friends, too?

The messengers stood up, ready to go outside, but Lot stopped them.

"Let me go talk to the people outside," he said, worried that they would do something wicked and cruel to God's messengers.

He went out of the house and talked to the crowd. "My friends, please leave my guests alone. They only stayed here because I asked. They will leave first thing tomorrow."

"All the more reason for us to get to know them now," said one man with an evil grin.

"Bring them out, Lot!" another man shouted. "It is not right for you to keep them all to yourself."

"Yes, bring them out!" the rest shouted even louder.

Lot did not know what to say anymore. He was getting scared. He had not expected this many people to be standing around his house or that they would be so angry. Could he protect God's messengers? Could he even protect himself?

Then the door of the house opened and God's messengers came out. Stretching their hands, they made the people in the crowd blind.

"My eyes!" a man shouted. "I can't see anything!"

"Why is everything so dark?" another wailed.

As they tripped and fell on top of each other, the messengers turned to Lot. "Take your family and leave this city at once, for this very night, God will destroy Sodom and Gomorrah."

Lot obeyed. He took his wife and two daughters and followed God's messengers out of the city.

"Hurry," they urged him as soon as they had walked past the city gates. "This is where we leave you, but you must not stop until you reach the mountain, and you must not look back even for a second so that you may be saved."

Lot kept walking, his wife and daughters a step behind him. Just after a few minutes, they started to complain.

"I can't walk another step," one of his daughters complained. "I'm tired, and my feet are hurting."

"I'm sleepy," the other one said with a yawn. "Can't we stop and rest until the sun comes up?"

"No," Lot answered. "We have to keep going."

"Do we really have to?" his wife complained. "Where are we even going? And why are we in such a hurry? We left behind so many of our things."

"Less talking and more walking," Lot scolded her. "Let us just get to the mountain as soon as possible."

No sooner had Lot and his family reached the mountains did God open the sky and throw down balls of fire. Sodom and Gomorrah were burned to the ground.

Lot heard the explosions and the distant screams. He smelled the smoke in the air.

"Father, what is going on?" one of his daughters asked in fear.

"Don't look back!" Lot shouted, remembering the warning of the messengers. "Whatever you do, you must never look back."

But his wife was too curious.

"I will just take a small peek," she thought before turning her head. The moment she did, she turned into a pillar of salt.

One of Lot's daughters saw this and screamed. "Mother!"

"Don't look back!" Lot repeated his warning.

He could hear only three pairs of footsteps now, and from listening to the cries of his daughter, he knew what had happened. Later, he would mourn for his wife, but for now, he had his children to take care of.

By morning, the wicked cities of Sodom and Gomorrah were nothing more but ashes. Only Lot and his daughters survived because they escaped. They stayed in a cave in the mountains, starting a new life under God's protection and guidance.

Abraham's Test

Many people don't live up to a hundred years old, but Abraham did. And what did he get? Not a birthday cake. Not a birthday hat. But he did receive the greatest gift of all - a child. God gave him a son just as He had promised.

His wife, Sarah, was even happier now that she was a mother, just like she had always dreamed of. She could not stop smiling as she carried her bundle of joy in her arms.

"I still can't believe we are parents now," she told Abraham. "And to such a cute boy, too."

"He is God's miracle," Abraham agreed as he held his son. "We are both old, yet here we are, blessed with the son we have always wanted."

"Now, the other women will no longer laugh at me," Sarah said. "It is our son who will laugh when he hears the story of how God gave him to us. He will laugh at me because I did not believe it was possible."

"Then we shall name him 'Isaac'," Abraham said. "Because that means 'he will laugh'. And I do hope he will have many things to laugh about in his life."

Isaac was a happy child, and Abraham and Sarah loved watching him grow. They liked watching him run with the sheep and dancing around the goats, but what Sarah did not like was seeing Isaac playing with Ishmael, Abraham's other son with their servant, Hagar.

One night, she spoke to Abraham.

"Husband," she said. "Do you remember when you told me that Hagar was going to have your child?"

Abraham nodded. "Yes."

"I was heartbroken then, but I said nothing. I had no right to complain because I could not give you a son. But now, we have Isaac. Shouldn't you send Hagar and Ishmael away?"

Abraham frowned. "But Ishmael is still my son," he reminded Sarah.

"And I am your wife," Sarah told him. "So one day, everything that you have will be Isaac's. Do you really want Ishmael to watch that happen? Do you want him and Isaac to fight when you are gone?"

Abraham understood why Sarah was concerned, and he wanted her and Isaac to be happy, but he still did not think it was right to send Ishmael away. He prayed to

God. "Dear God, please tell me what I must do so that everyone around me can be happy."

"It will be alright," God answered him. "Just take care of Sarah and Isaac, and send Hagar and Ishmael away. I will watch over them and make sure they live well."

So Abraham sent Hagar and Ishmael away, giving them bread and water for their journey. And God watched over them. When their water had run out, God led them to a well with plenty of water, and when they had no food, he helped Ishmael hunt. In time, Ishmael would grow up to be a good man and start over with his own family.

As for Isaac, he continued to grow. He had a strong body and a kind heart. Abraham and Sarah gave him everything he needed, and he obeyed them, not causing any trouble. They were a happy family, and God was happy to watch them, too, but he still had one final test left for Abraham, the hardest one of all.

One night, as Abraham was sleeping, God called his name. "Abraham."

"I'm here," Abraham answered as he got up.

"Tomorrow, take your son, Isaac, your only son whom you love with all your heart, and offer him up to me on the mountain."

Abraham could not believe his ears. He knew what offering something to God meant - a burnt sacrifice. He had made many offerings to God before - crops, goats, lambs. Now, God wants him to offer up his son, his only son?

Abraham wanted to say no, but he said nothing, going back to sleep.

Early the next morning, he woke Isaac up. "Wake up, my son, for I need you to come with me to the mountain. There, we will make an offering to God for everything he has done for us."

"But the sun is not even out yet." Isaac rubbed his eyes. "Do I really have to go, father?"

"Yes," Abraham answered. "It is what God wishes."

"Alright." Isaac sat up. "I will go with you."

Abraham brought two servants as well and plenty of wood for the offering. For three days, they journeyed to the mountain, Abraham mostly quiet along the way.

"Is something wrong, Father?" Isaac asked.

"Nothing," Abraham would answer. "I am just tired."

Then he would look away, unable to look at his son. How could he tell Isaac about God's request? How could any father tell his son that he was going to be a sacrifice?

On the third day, they reached the foot of the mountain. Abraham got off his donkey.

"Isaac and I will climb the mountain alone," he told his servants. "So stay here and wait."

"Yes, master," they replied.

Then Abraham gave Isaac the bunch of wood for the offering. "Come," he told his son. "Let us go up the mountain and worship God."

Isaac obeyed, following his father up the mountain. When they had reached a good spot for an offering, he asked his father what he should do.

"Arrange the wood into an altar," Abraham told him. "And I will start a fire."

Isaac obeyed, but when he was done, he was confused.

"Father," he said. "We have the altar and the fire, but where is the sacrifice? Did we forget to bring one?"

Abraham did not answer at once. He wanted to tell Isaac the truth, but he did not want his son to feel scared.

"God will provide the sacrifice, my son," he said as he tried to keep his voice from shaking. "For God is always merciful."

"You are right," Isaac agreed. "He gave me to you and mother, after all."

And now, God was going to take Isaac away, Abraham thought, feeling very sad that he was about to cry, but he held back his tears and turned to Isaac with a smile.

"Why don't you take a nap while we wait for the sacrifice, my son?" he said, running his hands through Isaac's hair. "Surely, you are tired from climbing the mountain."

"Alright," Isaac said.

Isaac lay on the ground, and after a few minutes, he fell asleep. Abraham watched him sleep, thinking that he looked so peaceful. He had no clue about what was going to happen, which only broke Abraham's heart all the more. He thought of asking God to spare Isaac, to ask something else from him, anything else. He was even willing to give up his life for his son. But in the end, he decided to trust God and obey.

He tied Isaac's hands, waking the boy up.

"Father?" Isaac's eyes grew wide with confusion and fear. "What is going on?"

Abraham did not answer, making Isaac wonder if he was in a nightmare. Surely, that's what it was because he knew his father loved him and would never cause him any harm.

Abraham, however, knew it was real, and his heart was heavy as he tied Isaac's hands and then his feet. Then he carried his son to the altar and put him down on top of the pile of wood just like he used to put Isaac on his bed. Tears blurred his vision as he took the knife from his side and lifted it, ready to sacrifice his son.

"Father?" Isaac felt even more confused. He could see the knife, and he began to tremble in fear.

"I'm sorry, my boy," Abraham said. Then he closed his eyes and tightened his grip on the knife in his hands as he prepared to strike.

Suddenly, a loud voice rumbled through the air. "Stop, Abraham!"

Abraham immediately froze. He knew the voice was God's.

"Do not harm the child," God ordered. "I know now that you fear me and will do whatever I ask, so there is no need for you to offer up your son to me. Release him."

Abraham let go of the breath he had been holding. Quickly, he untied Isaac and hugged him tightly.

"My son," he said with fresh tears in his eyes. "My beloved son."

Then he looked at Isaac. "Are you alright?"

Isaac nodded. "What happened, Father?"

"Nothing," Abraham said as he cupped his son's cheeks. "Think of it as just a bad dream."

Isaac looked at the altar. "But what about our offering?"

Just then, they heard a sound coming from a nearby bush. When they checked, they found a wild ram trapped there.

Abraham smiled. "Like I said, God is always merciful."

They caught the ram, placed it on the altar, and offered it to God. And God spoke to Abraham once more.

"Abraham, I know this was not an easy test, but you passed. As your reward, I will bless you with as many descendants as the stars in the sky and the grains of sand on the seashore, and they will tower over their enemies and rule over the nations."

Abraham and Isaac returned home safely, back to Sarah who was waiting for them, and Isaac would continue to grow into a fine man. Later, he would marry the woman God and Abraham chose for him - Rebekah.

The Winning Twin

I saac and his wife, Rebekah, were married for many years, but like Sarah, Rebekah could not seem to have a child.

"Each year, I get older, and still, I have not been able to give you a child," she told Isaac with a frown one evening. "If only I could have just one son like your mother did, I wouldn't ask for anything more."

Isaac wanted a child as well, so he prayed to God. "Dear God, I know you promised my father many descendants, and I believe that one day, you will give my wife many children, but if you could give her just one right now, it would make us both very happy."

God heard Isaac's prayer and His heart was moved. Weeks later, Rebekah discovered some very exciting news.

"Isaac, I'm pregnant!" she told him. "We are both finally going to be parents!"

"We are?" Isaac hugged his wife. "Thank God for his mercy."

Rebekah was very grateful and happy at first, too, but as the weeks passed by, her belly just kept getting bigger and bigger, even bigger than she thought it would be. Why, her belly was so big she was starting to wonder if she was carrying an elephant or a hippo and not a baby boy.

"There must be something wrong," she thought. "Surely, my belly is not supposed to be this big."

One night, when she could not sleep, she spoke to God.

"Dear God, I am thankful for this gift you have given me," Rebekah said. "But can you please tell me why it feels so strange? Is this really a baby boy I am carrying?"

"You are carrying not just one baby boy but two," God told her. "You and Isaac are having twins, two boys who will each grow up to become the father of a nation."

"Two?" Rebekkah almost screamed in surprise. No wonder her belly felt so heavy. But at least, she was not carrying an elephant.

"They will be brothers yet two very different persons," God continued. "They will each have their own strengths, but one will be stronger."

The months passed, and when the time came, Rebekah did give birth to twins. Some twins look exactly alike that even their moms and dads have a hard time telling them apart, but not Rebekah's twins. The one who came out first was covered in hair while the second with pale, smooth skin. Isaac named the first Esau and the second one Jacob.

As they grew up, it became even more clear how different the brothers were. Esau liked to be outdoors. He was strong and he liked to work on the fields and to hunt, which gained Isaac's approval. Jacob, on the other hand, preferred to stay inside the tent and read while his mother cooked or sewed, the two of them spending lots of time together. As a result, the two brothers drifted apart.

One afternoon, Esau came home from the fields dripping in sweat. It had been a hot day, and now, he was tired and his stomach was rumbling from hunger. In fact, he was so tired, he felt as if he was just going to fall over and pass out. When he saw Jacob eating a bowl of red beans, his mouth began to water.

"Let me have that," Esau said, trying to get the bowl from Jacob's hands. "I am starving and I need to get my strength back before I pass out."

Jacob, however, held on more tightly to his bowl. "It's mine," he said. "I got it first."

"Please," Esau begged. "I don't mind if you've already eaten from it. Just give me the rest."

"And what will you give me in return?" Jacob wondered. "You already have so much more than me. You are strong, while I am weak. As the older son, you will get all of our father's lands, while I will have nothing."

"What do you want?" Esau asked.

"I want your birthright," Jacob answered. "Whatever our father owns which he plans on giving to you, you will give to me."

Esau frowned. He did not like the sound of that, but he did not like the growing ache in his stomach more.

"Fine," he said, eyeing the bowl in his brother's hands. "Everything father owns will be of no use to me anyway if I get sick. Now, give me the bowl."

Jacob still did not give it. "Promise me first that you will give me your birthright."

Esau sighed. "I promise. Now, are you going to give me that bowl of food?"

This time, Jacob gladly handed the bowl over, watching Esau gobble up the food down to the very last bean and last drop of soup. Then Esau left.

The years passed. When Isaac was already very old, he called Esau to his tent.

"My son," Isaac said. "Since I am already very old, I may die any day, and I don't want that to happen without giving you my blessing, so please go and hunt a deer for me and serve me its cooked meat. After I eat, I will give you my blessing."

Esau nodded. "Yes, Father."

He left the tent, eager to go hunting right away, but little did he know that his mother had been standing outside the tent, and she also heard what Isaac had just said.

As soon as Esau was gone, Rebekah ran to find her younger son.

"Jacob!" she shouted. "Get up!"

"What is it, Mother?" Jacob asked without much interest.

"Your father is about to give Esau his blessing," Rebekah said. "But not if you get it first."

"Me?" Jacob's eyebrows crinkled. "How?"

"Just do as I say." Rebekah pulled Jacob off his bed and pushed him out of the tent. "Go and get me two young goats right now. I will prepare it just how your father likes it, and you will bring it to him."

"But won't he see through everything?" Jacob asked. "Surely, he will be able to tell that I am not Esau."

"Your father can hardly see now so he won't know," Rebekah answered.

"But if he gives me his blessing, he will touch my arms," Jacob said. "And he will know I am not Esau because my skin is smooth, and he will get angry and put a curse on me and not his blessing."

Rebekah sighed. "Stop whining and grow up. Your father will not put a curse on you, but if he does get angry, then I will take the blame. Now, go get me those goats."

Jacob did as his mother told him, and when he came back, Rebekah made the goat meat into a delicious meal, one of Isaac's favorites, then she put the hairy goat skin around Jacob's neck and arms. She also got one of Esau's clothes and made Jacob wear it.

"Now, your father will not know you are not Esau," she said. "So go to him and get his blessing."

Jacob went to his father's tent carrying the dish his mother had lovingly prepared.

"I'm back, Father," he said in his best imitation of Esau's deep voice.

"Who is it?" Isaac asked, hearing the voice.

"Who else would it be?" Jacob answered. "It's your first-born son, Esau, with the meat you asked for."

Isaac was surprised. "You were able to hunt and cook a deer so quickly?"

"It is because I had God's help," Jacob said.

Still, Isaac felt confused. The voice he could hear sounded like Jacob's, after all.

"Come closer, my son, that I might hug you," Isaac said.

Jacob obeyed and stretched out his arms. As Isaac hugged him, he felt the goat hair on Jacob's arms. He also smelled Esau's clothes, which smelled of a hard day's work in the field.

"This must really be Esau," he thought.

So he ate the food Jacob had brought him, and when he was done, he placed his hand on Jacob's head and gave his blessing.

"May God bless all your days that you may always have good harvests and never go hungry. May all the nations bow before you and honor you. May your relatives serve you. May your enemies be cursed and your friends be blessed."

Then Jacob left.

After a few hours, Esau returned.

"I have brought the meat you asked for, father," he said.

Once more, Isaac felt surprised and confused. "Didn't you already do that a while ago? I have already given you my blessing, haven't I?"

Esau himself could not understand what was going on. "What do you mean you have already given me your blessing? I, Esau, have been hunting all this time like you told me to and have only just returned."

Isaac frowned. "Then I must have given my blessing to someone else pretending to be you."

It did not take either of them long to figure out who that person was. There was only one other person who could have wanted the blessing, after all - Jacob.

Esau frowned. Not only did Jacob steal his birthright but also his father's blessing, and now, there was nothing left for him.

"So my little brother has won and taken everything that is mine," Esau said, sighing.

Indeed, Jacob had lived up to his name, which meant 'to go for something beyond reach' or 'take someone else's place'.

Esau felt very angry. In fact, he wanted to fight his younger brother, but he told himself he would wait until his father was gone and the period of mourning for him was over.

Rebekah learned of this, so she told Jacob to pack his things and leave.

"Your brother hates you now," she said. "So go and stay with my brother until his anger has passed."

Jacob left, and for many years, he traveled far from home. With God's guidance, he found two wives and had children. His father-in-law gave him many things, too, making him rich, but he still yearned for home, and he wanted to see his father and mother again. He was scared of Esau, of course, but he decided to be brave. He knew God was with him, after all.

Bringing many gifts, Jacob headed home, sending messengers ahead of him to let Esau know of his coming. The day before he was supposed to meet Esau, he asked God for guidance and protection.

"Dear God, years ago, you came to me in a dream and promised me the same thing you promised my grandfather, Abraham - that you would bless me and give me many children and grandchildren. Now, however, I am scared that my brother will ask me to fight him and defeat me. I know I do not deserve your protection because I was the one who made him angry, but please protect me."

God heard Jacob's prayer. That night, as Jacob was about to sleep, he saw a stranger who challenged him to a fight with bare hands. Jacob recognized the stranger as God's messenger and he accepted the challenge, wrestling with the messenger all night. The messenger was strong, but Jacob did not give up. When dawn came, the fight remained a draw.

"Let us end here," the messenger said. "For you have already won the grace of God. As your reward, you will have a new name - Israel."

Israel went to meet Esau, and seeing his older brother with his army, he bowed before Esau and asked for his forgiveness. As soon as Esau saw his younger brother, his anger disappeared. They embraced each other as they wept tears of joy.

"Welcome home, brother," Esau said. "It's been a long time."

As different as Jacob and Esau were and as many disagreements as they had in the past, they were still brothers, so they decided to stop fighting and forgive each other. The time for competing was over. Now, it was time to get along, which they did even after Isaac passed away, mourning his loss together.

Egypt Gets Punished

J acob - or Israel - did become the father of a nation, the citizens of which were called Israelites. Like other nations, Israel had problems - war, famine, sickness. The Israelites traveled far in search of better lives, and many of them ended up in the land of Egypt as slaves.

Everyday, they worked under the burning sun carrying heavy bricks on their backs to make the pyramids. Some cleaned the houses of the Egyptians and did the cooking and took care of the children. Others worked in the fields. All of this they did without getting paid, receiving only a bit of food and a mat to sleep in.

Day and night, the Israelites would cry out, "God, save us. Help us get back home to the land of our ancestors."

God heard His people's cries, but in order to save them, He needed a hero. He needed a good man who would listen to His word and carry out His works.

Finally, after hundreds of years, that hero arrived.

Moses was not like any other Israelite in Egypt. He was not a slave. Rather, he grew up in the Egyptian palace. Now that he had left, though, he was working as a shepherd.

One day, while he was taking care of his sheep, he saw a baffling sight. Imagine his surprise when he saw a bush that was covered in flames and yet it wasn't actually burning, the leaves still green and no smoke rising in the air. He tried to take a closer look, but as soon as he had taken a step, a voice stopped him in his tracks.

"Moses!" the voice called.

Moses was startled. He looked around but he could not see anyone around. Who was calling his name?

"Moses!" the voice spoke again, and this time, Moses nearly jumped.

It was the not-burning-bush that was talking! Or was it?

"I am the God of Abraham, Isaac, and Jacob, your ancestors," the voice said.

Moses was in awe. He could hardly believe what he had heard, but he knew the bush was proof of how extraordinary the moment was. He took off his shoes and bowed his head.

God spoke again. "I have been waiting for someone to set my people free, and finally, I have found someone suitable. You will bring the Israelites out of Egypt into a land of their own, a peaceful and prosperous land."

Moses' eyebrows crumpled. "Me?"

"Yes, Moses," God answered. "You will go back to the palace and stand before the Pharaoh, the king of Egypt, so that I may speak and act through you."

Moses' eyes grew wide. "But I am just an ordinary man, and the Pharaoh is the most powerful man in all of Egypt."

"You can bring your brother, Aaron, with you if that will make you feel braver," God told him. "But you must not worry about what you will say because I will give you the words. And do not worry if the Pharaoh does not listen, which is exactly what he will do, because I will be the one to teach him and Egypt a lesson."

Moses called his brother, Aaron, and asked to see the Pharaoh. The guards let him in, but the Pharaoh was not happy to see him.

"What do you want?" the Pharaoh asked Moses. "I thought you said you were never coming back here to the palace."

"I am not here for me but for the God of Israel," Moses answered. "He wants you to set his people free."

The Pharaoh laughed. "Who is this god? Why does he think he has the right to tell me what to do? If he really is very powerful, let him prove it."

Following God's command, Moses turned to Aaron. "Let go of the rod in your hand," he said to his brother.

Aaron did that. As soon as the rod hit the floor, it turned into a snake.

The Pharaoh laughed once more. "Is that all your god can do? My priests can do the same."

And his priests threw their rods on the floor, and they, too, turned into snakes. Aaron's snake was the largest, swallowing all of the other snakes up before turning back into a rod, but the Pharaoh did not care.

"I will not let the Israelites go," he said.

The next day, Moses and Aaron stood before Pharaoh once more.

"The God of Israel is ordering you to let His people go," they said again.

Pharaoh refused, so Aaron stood by the edge of the river and dipped his rod into the water, and it turned red. The water had turned into blood!

All over Egypt, the people could not drink. They could not wash their clothes or their bodies. All the fish were unable to breathe as well.

The Pharaoh was amazed, and he was concerned, but he still refused to give in to Moses and Aaron.

"I will not let the Israelites go," he said.

After seven days, the waters turned back. Moses and Aaron returned to Pharaoh.

"The God of Israel wants you to let His people go," they said.

"And what will he do if I don't?" the Pharaoh asked.

"He will send frogs upon Egypt," Moses answered. "Hundreds of them."

The Pharaoh snorted. "I am not afraid of frogs."

So Moses told Aaron to stretch his rod over the streams and ponds, and out of the water, hundreds of frogs jumped out. They croaked and they jumped all over the place. They filled every home, covering the beds so the Egyptians couldn't sleep and sitting inside the ovens so that the Egyptians could not cook. They even climbed over the Egyptians, sticking to their clothes.

After Pharaoh had to remove a slimy frog from his head, he called Moses and Aaron, huffing and puffing.

"Take the frogs away right now, and I will let the Israelites go," he said.

As soon as God gave the command, the frogs stopped moving. The Egyptians swept them into piles, covering their noses as they did. There were so many dead frogs that they almost made a mountain - a stinky, slimy mountain that was.

Still, the Pharaoh was glad to see the frogs gone, and now that they were not croaking in his ear and jumping everywhere, his mind was clear again.

"I will not let the Israelites go," he said.

As punishment, God ordered Aaron to stretch out his rod, and the dust rose from the ground and turned into lice - those tiny insects that give itchy bites and hide in hair. The lice made nests in the hairs of the Egyptians, who scratched their heads day and night and covered their skin in bites. They covered the animals, too, many of which fell very sick.

Still, the Pharaoh refused to let go of the Israelite slaves.

So God unleashed swarms of flies. They buzzed around the Egyptians' ears every second of the day, and they covered all the food.

When Pharaoh saw the flies floating in his bath, he called Moses and Aaron.

"Go pray to your god," he said. "And ask him to get rid of all these pesky, disgusting flies, then I will let the Israelites go."

God did get rid of all the flies, every single one of them, but as soon as they were gone, the Pharaoh changed his mind once more.

"I will not let the Israelites go," he said.

After several days, Moses and Aaron stood before the Pharaoh once more.

"You must free the Israelites as God commands," they said. "Otherwise, a terrible sickness will fall upon the livestock in Egypt."

The Pharaoh refused, so the next day, the cows, the sheep, the goats, the donkeys and the camels in Egypt all fell sick and died. Only the animals owned by the Israelites survived.

This made the Pharaoh angry, and the more he refused to let the Israelites go, so next, God made the Egyptians suffer, covering their skin with boils and then sending a sickness upon them.

Still, the Pharaoh remained stubborn. "I don't care what this god of Israel will do," he said. "I am the most powerful man in Egypt and I bow to no one. I will not let the Israelites go."

Then God told Moses, "Point your rod towards the sky, and I will send down thunder and hail upon Egypt."

Moses obeyed. The skies rumbled. Drops of rain as hard and large as stones and balls of fire fell from the sky, hurting the Egyptians and making holes in their roofs. Even the fields burned and the trees fell. The Egyptians were so scared and they begged their king to help them, so the Pharaoh summoned Moses and Aaron.

"I have made a mistake which has led to the suffering of my people," he said. "Ask your god to stop this thunder and hail, and I will let your people go."

Moses prayed to God, and the sky fell silent and cleared. No more hail fell from the sky.

When the Pharaoh saw this, he laughed. "Ha! I have tricked your god once more. Did he really believe I would let his people go? I will not."

After a few more days, Moses and Aaron returned to the palace and stood before the Pharaoh.

"The God of Israel - "

"Wants me to let his people go," the Pharaoh finished, having already heard the demand too many times. "But like I said, I will not."

"Then God will send a storm of locusts upon Egypt," Moses said.

As soon as Moses stretched out his hand, a strong wind blew. With it came the locusts - grasshoppers that travel in swarms. The swarms were so big that they covered the sky. They ate every bit of green that was left, and the Egyptians, who by now had very little to eat, had nothing.

"We will not survive without food," they wailed. "Why won't our king just let the people of Israel go?"

So the Pharaoh called Moses and Aaron and said, "I am the one who must be punished, not my people, for I am the one who refused to let the people of Israel go, but if you ask your god to show mercy on my people, then I will show mercy on his."

Moses prayed to God, and a strong wind blew. It blew all the locusts out into sea where they drowned and disappeared, not a single one left.

"Now, let the people of Israel go," Moses told the Pharaoh after.

However, the Pharaoh changed his mind again.

God said to Moses, "This time, tell the Pharaoh I will punish Egypt by sending darkness over the land."

Moses sent the Pharaoh this message, and as soon as the Pharaoh had heard it, the sky turned from blue to gray to black. No one could see a thing!

The Egyptians tried to find their way in the darkness, but they ended up stumbling and tripping. They could not even see their hands or feet. Many decided to just sit still in their homes, trembling in fear.

Even the Pharaoh felt scared. Every now and then, he would feel a shiver go up his spine because he did not know what could be walking around in the darkness. What if there was a monster in the room? Or an assassin? He wanted to call for Moses and Aaron and ask them to end the dark spell, but since no one could see anything, he had to wait.

After three days, the darkness left. Finally, the Pharaoh could talk to Moses and Aaron.

"I have had enough of these punishments," he said. "Your people may go, even the children, but leave behind your horses and your cows and your sheep, for my people have nothing left to eat."

Moses shook his head. "If we are going, we will take all our animals with us and not one will be left behind."

The Pharaoh frowned. "Then you cannot go! How dare you say no to me when I've already granted your wish! Now, get out of my sight!"

Moses left, sighing.

"What a stubborn king," he thought. "God has already sent many punishments upon Egypt - the river of blood, the frogs, the lice, the flies, the sicknesses upon both the animals and the people, the thunder and hail, the locusts and the darkness. What else does God have to do to soften his heart and convince him to willingly let Israel go?"

In his throne, the Pharaoh laughed. "I will never let the Israelites go," he said. "Not after everything they have done to Egypt. There is nothing more their god can do to make me change my mind."

Little did he know that God already had something planned - the biggest punishment of all - that would bring even the greatest king down on his knees.

A Path Through The Sea

One day, God said to Moses, "Tell my people that there will be a feast later this month. They have to prepare a young male goat or sheep, and on the day of the celebration, they will use some of its blood to mark the doorposts of their houses. Then they shall roast it whole and eat its meat with bitter vegetables and flatbread. While they eat, they shall stay inside the house but with their shoes on. They must be ready to go on a journey, for that very night, I will pass through Egypt and strike down every firstborn child of man and beast as a final punishment, but I will pass over the houses of the Israelites that are marked with blood, and they shall be spared."

Moses told the Israelites everything God had told him, and their eyes grew wide as they gasped.

"God will take the lives of all the firstborn Egyptians?" they asked. "Then will we finally be free?"

"God said that after this punishment, the Pharaoh will let you all go," Moses answered. "Which is why on that night, you must be ready to leave in a hurry. Pack everything you need and put on your traveling clothes, even your shoes."

"Are you sure our children will be spared?" a woman asked, pressing her baby close to her heart.

"God will pass over every house marked with blood," Moses said. "Which is why the feast will be called the Lord's Passover."

The Israelites were excited. Some of them jumped for joy. Others began to sing and dance. Others still raised their hands and praised God. For years, they had prayed for God to save them, and now, finally, their prayers had been answered. Soon, they would be free - free to work their own fields, take care of their own families, and eat and sleep whenever they wanted. They could not wait for the feast of the Passover.

Finally, the day came. The Israelites prepared their feast and marked their doorposts, then at night, they locked themselves inside their houses as they ate.

At midnight, God passed by every house in Egypt. Whenever He saw a door with red markings on either side of it, He did not go inside that house, instead passing over and leaving everyone in the house alone. However, He entered every door without the markings, and when He left, He took the lives of every firstborn in that house with Him.

"No!" an Egyptian woman screamed when she realized the child in her arms was no longer breathing. "What happened to my son? He was fine just a moment ago, but now, I can no longer hear his heart beating."

The other women checked on their children and found that their firstborns had stopped breathing as well, and they began to cry. Even the firstborns of the servants were not spared, nor were every firstborn animal, be it cow, sheep, or cat.

All the wails woke the Pharaoh up, and he was about to ask someone what was going on, when a servant came to him, crying.

"The prince is gone," she said.

The Pharaoh was confused. "What do you mean the prince is gone? Did someone take him?"

The servant did not answer, sobbing in her hands.

Worried, the Pharaoh ran to his son's room. He saw his son lying in the middle of his big bed, and he felt relieved. That was until he noticed that his son's chest didn't seem to be moving.

He went to the bed and shook his son. "Wake up!"

But the boy would not open his eyes.

The Pharaoh pressed his ear to his son's chest, and when he could not hear any sound, it was as if his whole world had stopped and shattered at the same time.

What the servant said was true. His beloved son, the first prince of Egypt who was supposed to take his place as Pharaoh one day, was gone.

"My son!" the Pharaoh cried.

The rest of his family, the servants, and the guards cried with him, the cries of the Egyptians filling the air, for everyone had just lost someone - a son, a daughter, a father, a mother, a brother, a sister.

His eyes still red, the Pharaoh called for Moses and Aaron.

"Take your people and all your cows and your sheep and go," he told them. "Now that my son is gone, your god has won. Get out of my sight and my land and never return!"

The Egyptians, too, pulled the Israelites out of their homes and pushed them away.

"You have taken everything from us!" they shouted angrily. "Go with your god and leave us alone!"

The Israelites left Egypt, bringing everything they owned, including their animals. They even brought the bones of their ancestor, Joseph, who was the youngest son of Jacob and one of the first Israelites to live in Egypt long before they became slaves.

As they walked, they could not stop smiling or singing praises to God.

"Oh, I wish I could have seen the look on the Pharaoh's face," one of them said.

"Who cares about the Pharaoh?" another answered. "We are free! God has delivered us from Egypt!"

God led the people of Israel through the wilderness, and He stayed with them, appearing as a cloud during the day.

"Why is that cloud always following us?" a child asked his mother.

"It is God," the mother answered. "He is always with us, His people."

At night, God appeared as a glowing pillar of fire, lighting the way of the Israelites.

"It is so beautiful," a woman said.

"And bright enough to scare the wolves," her husband said. "And warm enough to keep the chill away, too. Truly, God is with us."

The Israelites walked for days, following Moses. They were getting tired, their knees and their feet starting to hurt.

"How much further do we have to walk?" one of them asked. "We have been carrying heavy loads for years. Our bodies cannot take more of this."

"Hush," someone told him. "Quit complaining. Don't you know that God is listening? You know what He did to the Egyptians. Do you want to be punished also?"

The man stopped complaining, but there were other people who started grumbling, and children who started crying.

God noticed this, and He said to Moses, "Tell the Israelites that they can set up a camp at the edge of the wilderness near the sea so that everyone can rest."

Moses told the people this, and they gladly put up their tents and their feet.

Meanwhile, back in Egypt, the mood was still sour. The Egyptians had lost so much - their loved ones, their food, their fields, and animals. Even the Pharaoh was still grieving for his son and his pride still stung from his defeat.

"We should never have taken Israelites for slaves," he complained. "Look at all the trouble they have caused us."

"Wrong," one of his advisers said. "We should never have let them go. Look at Egypt now. It is falling apart. We have lost so many people and many fields and buildings have been destroyed. How will we rebuild without our slaves? How will we continue building the pyramids?"

"We barely have any animals left," another adviser pointed out. "We should at least have forced the Israelites to leave their herds and flocks behind."

"They would not leave without their animals," the Pharaoh said. "And I could not stand the sight of them any longer. If I had not let them go, who knows what their god will do next? Punish all the children? All the men? All the women? Then there will be no Egyptian left."

"As it stands, the remaining Egyptians may not survive," an adviser said, sighing.

The Pharaoh scratched his head. "What do you think I should do then?"

"Go after the Israelites and bring them back," another adviser said. "I have already sent some soldiers to follow them, and they seem to have set up camp between the wilderness and the sea. They have nowhere to go, so it is the perfect place to strike. Maybe some of them will jump into the ocean and some of them will scatter into the wilderness where they will be chased by wild animals, but if we go after them now, we can capture most of them."

The other advisers nodded.

"We do not need them all back," one said. "If we get a few hundred slaves and a few herds of cattle and flocks of sheep, we will be fine."

"It will be easier than getting new slaves somewhere else," another said.

The Pharaoh thought about everything his advisers had said, and after a while, he made up his mind. He had already lost his son anyway, what more did he have to lose?

"Get the chariots and soldiers ready," he ordered, standing from his throne. "We will go after the Israelites!"

Following the Pharaoh, the army of Egypt chased after the Israelites, and since they were riding horses and chariots, they reached the camp of the Israelites in just a day.

As soon as the people of Israel felt the ground shaking, they knew that the Egyptians had come after them, and they were scared. When they heard the horses and saw the sunlight bouncing off the shiny chariots, they panicked.

"What will we do?" they asked. "Have we been freed from Egypt just to suffer a worse fate?"

"Should we go into the wilderness or jump into the sea?"

"Has God abandoned us?"

"We should just surrender and go back to Egypt," some of them said. "Slavery is better than nothing."

Moses saw them running around, and he heard their cries.

"Stay calm!" he urged them. "Why are you so afraid? God saved you from Egypt, did he not? Have you forgotten how God has shown His power to the Egyptians? Be at peace, for God will fight for His people."

Then Moses prayed. "Dear God, tell me what I should do."

"Stretch your rod over the sea," God ordered. "And I shall make a path."

Moses did as he was told. He stood on the cliff and stretched his rod over the sea, and behold, the waters parted, forming walls on either side of a dry path.

The Israelites were amazed.

"Did God just order the sea to cut itself in half?" they wondered.

"Don't just stare!" one of them shouted. "Let's go cross before the Egyptians capture us or the sea goes back the way it was."

The Israelites carried whatever they could and followed the sandy path through the sea. They had to be careful not to step on the coral or on the scurrying crabs that didn't seem to understand what was going on either.

As for the other sea animals, they were all safe in the water. The sharks behaved, not showing their sharp teeth. The octopuses lent an arm, or two, or eight, in helping to carry heavy bags. One even shook a child's hand.

"Look, Mommy!" The child pointed at the octopus. "I found a new friend."

His mother grabbed his hand. "Now is not the time to be making friends. We must hurry to the other side."

When the Pharaoh saw the Israelites crossing the sea, he ordered his soldiers to chase after them.

"Don't let them escape!" he shouted. "If they can cross the sea, so can we."

However, the wheels of their chariots and the hooves of the horses were too heavy, and they got stuck in the sand. The soldiers had to run after the Israelites, but their feet kept sinking into the sand as well. The fact that the crabs pinched their toes and the squids sprayed ink on their faces slowed them down, too.

After several hours, the Israelites were able to make it across the sea. The Egyptians, on the other hand, were moving more and more slowly, getting tired with every step.

"Maybe we should just turn around and go back," they said.

Some of them did just that, the others pushing forward. The Pharaoh simply stood on the cliff, watching them. He, too, was torn about what he should tell his soldiers to do.

Moses, on the other hand, knew exactly what to do. He stood on the cliff on the other side, and when all the Israelites had safely crossed the sea, he stretched his hand over the sea just as he had done earlier.

At once, the walls of the sea formed large waves that crashed into each other, the waters merging into one. The Egyptian soldiers and their horses and chariots were all swallowed up by the sea. Not a single one was left.

The Israelites praised God. "God has saved us not once but twice," they said. "Let us all rejoice!"

"God is our strength," they sang. "He has paved a path for us through the sea and drowned all of our enemies."

Some of them still could not believe what had just happened, but they chose to believe in Moses and in God.

"We will serve God and go wherever He tells us to," they said.

The Israelites continued their journey, following Moses to the promised land.

The Amazing Slingshot

S words, spears, bows and arrows, magic wands, cat-apults. These are usually the weapons that bring down giants and monsters and win battles that go down in history. But did you know that one boy was able to take down a giant with just a piece of wood, a string of rope, and a pebble?

This happened during the time of Saul, the first king of Israel. There was also a great prophet who lived then - Samuel, who God had called to serve Him since he was still a boy.

One night, God spoke to Samuel. "Go to Bethlehem and find the man named Jesse. One of his seven sons will be the true king of Israel."

Samuel did not want to go. "Israel already has a king," he said.

"But Saul has turned away from me," God answered. "Israel needs a better king, a good king."

Samuel sighed. "When Saul hears I have anointed another king, he will be angry, and he will get rid of this new king."

"Then do not tell him or anyone," God said. "Go to Jesse and ask him to gather his sons so that together, you all may offer a sacrifice to me. I will tell you who I have chosen once he is standing in front of you, and you will pour the oil over his head, and I will give him my blessing."

Samuel went to Bethlehem and asked Jesse to help him prepare a sacrifice for the Lord. He also asked Jesse to call his sons.

"I've heard you have seven sons," Samuel said. "Why don't you invite them to join us so that they may also make a sacrifice to God and receive his blessing?"

Jesse called his sons, and one by one, they stood before Samuel to receive God's blessing.

The oldest son, Eliab, came first, of course. He was also very tall and looked very strong. When he stood in front of Samuel, Samuel thought, "He looks like a king so he must be God's chosen one."

But God said, "I do not look at men's appearances. I look into their hearts. This is not my chosen one."

So Samuel moved to the second son, but God also had not chosen him. The third, fourth, fifth and sixth all stood in front of Samuel, but God had not chosen any of them.

"My chosen one is not here," God said.

Samuel turned to Jesse. "Where is your youngest son? You said you have seven, but I have only blessed six."

"My youngest son is working," Jesse answered. "Right now, he is in the meadow looking after the sheep."

"Send for him," Samuel ordered. "We will not start until he is here."

Jesse ordered a servant to fetch his youngest son, and soon, he arrived. He looked even younger than Samuel had expected, and his clothes were dirty from laying down with the sheep.

"Surely, this cannot be Israel's true king," Samuel thought.

Yet God said, "This is my chosen one, the future and true king of Israel."

As he stood before Samuel, Samuel asked him, "What is your name?"

"David," the boy answered.

Samuel took some oil and poured it over David's head, and from then on, God was with David.

King Saul, of course, did not know about all this. He continued to rule, trying to do a good job as king. But being king is definitely not easy, and one of the hardest tasks is winning a war.

When the Philistines declared war, Saul gathered his own army and went to the border, a big valley all that stood between the Israelites and the invaders.

"No matter what, we cannot let the Philistines cross the valley and invade our country," Saul said. "If they try, we will push them back and teach them a lesson."

The Israelites cheered upon hearing the brave words of their king, which was like music to Saul's ears, but all of a sudden, they became quiet. Just as Saul was about to ask why, he saw the reason for their silence and their fear - a Philistine on the other side of the valley standing almost ten feet tall. His large, brass helmet and thick armor glimmered in the sunlight, and he held his spear as if it was as light as a stick.

"Israelites!" he shouted. "I am Goliath of Gath, a Philistine, and I say there is no need for a war today. If anyone wishes to fight me, let him step forward. If he can defeat me, then we, the Philistines, will be your servants, but if I defeat him, then you, the Israelites, will serve us."

When Saul heard this, he thought it was wise. "There is no need for the valley to become a river of blood," he said to himself.

However, he was also afraid.

"I do not think there is any Israelite as big as that Goliath," he thought, stroking his beard. "If one of my soldiers fights against him, we will surely lose."

So Saul sat in his tent and worried about what he should do.

Each day, Goliath made his challenge, and each day, no Israelite stepped forward to fight him, Saul remaining in his tent.

Goliath sighed. "Is no Israelite brave enough to fight for his country?" he wondered.

Meanwhile, David continued to look after the sheep, but one day, his father called him.

"Go and bring food to your brothers who are camped near the valley," Jesse ordered.

David obeyed. Leaving the sheep in the care of another shepherd, he went to the soldiers' camp. As soon as he got there, he looked for his brothers, but it was Goliath who caught his eye.

"Won't anyone from Israel fight me?" Goliath bellowed, his voice thundering across the valley.

The soldiers around David trembled, some running away.

"I do not care if King Saul has promised great rewards for whoever beats that Philistine," one of them said. "I am not going to go and fight him."

"Me neither," another said. "He is too big and scary. Just look at his spear. It is bigger than me."

But David was not scared. "Who does that Philistine think he is?" he said. "It does not matter how big he is. He cannot stand against a soldier of God."

Eliab, his older brother, heard him and got mad. "What are you talking about? What are you even doing here? Shouldn't you be watching over the sheep?"

David sighed. Ever since Samuel had given him a special blessing, his brothers had been mean to him, but he tried not to mind.

"I have done nothing wrong," David said. "I am just telling the truth - that a Philistine cannot win against a soldier of God."

The Israelites began to murmur, and soon, David's words reached Saul in his tent. Curious, Saul called David.

"Are you saying that Philistine can be defeated?" Saul asked.

"Yes," David answered. "In fact, I will go and fight him myself, for I am not afraid."

Saul laughed. "You? Aren't you too young and too small for the battlefield? Do you even know how to fight?"

"I have fought a lion and a bear when they tried to eat my father's lambs," David said. "Just as God has saved me from that lion and that bear, God will protect me against that Philistine."

Saul was impressed with David's confidence, and there was something about the boy that told Saul he could win, so Saul nodded. "If God is with you and you want to fight, who am I to stop you?"

Because David had no armor, Saul lent the boy his own armor and helped him put it on, but it was too big, it looked like it would fall off him.

"I cannot wear this," David said, taking the armor off. "I have never worn armor before so I cannot fight in it."

Saul understood. He helped David out of the armor and then gave him a sword.

"At least, take a weapon," Saul said.

But David shook his head. "I already have a weapon."

He walked out of Saul's tent towards the battlefield with his slingshot in hand.

When the other soldiers saw David, they became scared for him.

"He is going to get hurt," they said. "That giant Philistine is going to squash him like a bug."

But David was not scared. He stood before Goliath with his head held high.

Goliath laughed. "Do you think this is some child's game? Go home, little boy."

The other Philistines laughed as well, but David remained standing.

Goliath sighed. "If you think I will hold back, I won't." Then he stepped forward. "Come, and I will defeat you in five seconds."

Still, David was not afraid.

"You have your weapon and your armor," he said. "But I have the protection and the power of the God of Israel, the one true god."

Goliath frowned. "Enough talking. Let us fight!"

Goliath ran towards David, his footsteps making the ground shake, but David did not run away. He reached into his bag for a pebble and placed it on his slingshot. Then he stretched the rope and let it go, sending the stone flying straight into Goliath's forehead. The giant stopped running. He touched his forehead, then in the next moment, he fell to the ground.

The Israelites cheered. The Philistines panicked and started running, scared of David and his god.

"After them!" Saul shouted, ordering his soldiers to chase down the Philistines and make sure they never came back.

Then he looked at the boy who had taken down Goliath.

"Who is that boy?" he asked his general.

The general shook his head. "I do not know, my king."

"Bring him to me," Saul ordered.

The general brought David before Saul, who gave him a pat on the shoulder.

"I did not know Israel had someone who could use a slingshot so well," Saul told him. "Will you tell me your name?"

"My name is David, my king," David replied.

Saul placed his hand on David's shoulder and smiled. "David, since you have defeated the Philistines, from this day on, you shall live with me in my palace, and I will treat you as my own son."

David bowed his head. "As you wish, my king."

Later, David himself would become king as God had planned and rule over Israel with God's wisdom and protection. He would be loved and remembered by his people, his star a symbol for Israel up until today.

The Worst Haircut

E very hero has a secret to their strength and a weakness. Samson was no different.

His story begins before he was born, when the Philistines invaded and conquered Israel. Because of this, many Israelites had to work as slaves of the Philistines.

Some of them began to lose hope. One was Manoah, whose wife could not give him any children.

"Maybe God has abandoned Israel," he thought sadly. "Every day, I have to work as a slave, and my wife cannot even give me any children."

Manoah did not know that God was listening.

One day, Manoah's wife was surprised to receive a message from God.

"Listen carefully to what God has planned for you," the messenger told her. "You will soon give birth to a son, and this boy will be stronger than any other, even the strongest Philistine, so long as you do not cut even a single lock of his hair."

Manoah's wife shook her head. "How can I believe something that is too good to be true?"

However, the messenger came to visit again, this time appearing to both Manoah and his wife.

"It must be true," Manoah said. "We will have a son, and Israel will finally have its savior."

Indeed, months later, Manoah's wife gave birth to a boy. They named him Samson.

Samson grew up handsome, healthy, and strong, and of course, with long locks of flowing hair. When the time came for him to marry, his parents were confident that the most beautiful women in Israel would line up to be his wife. They never expected Samson to disappoint them by choosing a Philistine woman.

"I have already given my heart to a beautiful Philistine woman," he said. "Tomorrow, I will ask her to give me hers and be my wife."

The next day, Samson left home. On his way to the town of the Philistines, he suddenly heard a rustle and a crackle of leaves.

"Danger is near," he thought.

Suddenly, a loud roar thundered in his ears. In the next moment, a large animal jumped out of the bushes. Was it a kangaroo? But no, it had a thick mane. Was it a baboon? Baboons didn't have sharp claws, though.

A thick mane and sharp claws? Wait. It was a lion!

It jumped at Samson, but Samson was quicker and stronger. He was able to overpower the beast and defeat it using just his hands.

Afterwards, he continued on his journey to see his would-be wife. She was thrilled to hear his marriage proposal, and she happily accepted it.

Samson smiled. "Then when I return, we will get married."

He went back home to tell his parents about the wedding. He took the same road so he saw the body of the lion he had slain. Bees had already made a home in its bones, busy making honey, which looked so glossy and smelled so sweet that Samson just had to try a dollop.

Afterwards, Samson licked his lips. "Mmm. This honey is the best treat I've ever had," he said

It also gave him an idea.

During his wedding feast, Samson gave his guests, who were mostly Philistines, a riddle.

"Out of the hunter came the meat and out of the strong came the sweet," he said. ""Answer my riddle within a week and I will give you thirty sets of clothes. If you cannot, then you have to give the clothes to me."

The Philistines scratched their beards and heads. What could this riddle mean?

As the days passed, the Philistines grew restless. They did not want to lose, so they spoke to Samson's wife.

"Make your husband tell you the answer to the riddle," they said. "Then tell us so that we don't have to give him anything."

The woman shook her head. "But Samson is my husband now," she said. "My loyalty is to him."

"Not if you don't want us to burn your father's house," they told her.

The woman had no choice. She had to get Samson to tell her the answer to the riddle.

"I thought a man should not keep any secrets from his wife," she said to him. "I am your wife now. Shouldn't you tell me everything, even the answer to the riddle?"

Samson did not want to, but he did love his wife, so he told her the answer. "The meat is the lion and the sweet is honey."

His wife told the Philistines this same thing, and they gave the answer back to Samson before the week was over.

As soon as they did, Samson knew he had been tricked.

"You forced my wife to give you the answer, didn't you?" he growled.

They just laughed. "Anyway, you lost, so give us thirty sets of clothes."

"Fine," Samson said, gritting his teeth.

He went out to get the clothes, then he decided to go back to his father's house, leaving his wife behind.

After some time, Samson returned to take his wife, but imagine his shock when he found out that she was already with another man.

"I thought you no longer wanted her," his father-in-law said. "So I gave her to another man. But please don't be angry. If you'd like, you can have her younger sister instead. She is even more beautiful."

Samson didn't like this at all. In fact, he became very angry.

"Just as I thought, the Philistines cannot be trusted," he thought to himself. "I let their trickery go last time, but this time, they will pay. They are the fools, not me."

Samson went and caught three hundred foxes. He tied blocks of wood to their tails, setting them on fire before setting the foxes free. The scared foxes ran in every direction, dragging the burning wood behind them. The cornfields, the vineyards, and the olive groves burned.

Seeing how their crops had turned to ashes, the Philistines became angry.

"Who did this and why?" they demanded to know.

"Samson," someone said. "Because he lost the Philistine woman who was supposed to be his wife."

Hearing this, the Philistines went to the house of Samson's father-in-law and burned it down. Samson's wife lost her life in the fire, and Samson's heart got even more broken.

"They have done it now," he said, and he went out and took down many Philistines to make them pay for what they had taken from him.

Then he went to Judah to spend some time alone.

The Philistines came to Judah looking for him. "If you don't hand Samson over, you will pay," they said to the people.

So the people went to Samson. "Are you a fool?" they asked him. "You know the Philistines are our masters. We don't know what you did to them, but now, we must hand you over to them, or we will also be in trouble."

They tied him up then brought him to the Philistines.

When the Philistines saw Samson tied up, they laughed, but as soon as Samson was standing in front of them, he used his strength to break the ropes like they were merely coils of thread. Then he picked up a bone that was lying around and struck down a thousand Philistines.

The Israelites cheered. Finally, there was one of them strong enough to stand up to the Philistines. God had sent them a hero!

The Philistines were worried, so they tried to get rid of Samson. They led him inside one of their cities and closed the gates while he slept, thinking that in the morning, an army of them would surround the city and take him down.

However, Samson knew what they were planning, and in the middle of the night, he got up and broke the gates, carrying the posts with him up to the mountains.

When the Philistine army arrived, they saw the gates broken, and their jaws dropped.

"Samson is a monster," they said. "Not a man."

From then on, the Philistines were too scared to even go near him, and they started to think of how they could take him down.

When they found out that Samson was in love again, this time with a woman named Delilah, they saw their chance.

They approached her with a proposal. "If you can help us take Samson down by discovering his weakness, we will give you more money than you have ever dreamed of."

Delilah liked the idea of money more than Samson, so she agreed.

When Samson came to her that night, she tried to act cold.

"What's wrong?" Samson asked her.

"Nothing," she said. "It just makes me feel uneasy that there are many things I don't know about you, like your weakness. I know you are strong, but I wonder what makes you weak."

"Is that all?" Samson chuckled. "Then I will tell you. My weakness is ropes, particularly new ones that have never been dried or used before."

As he slept, Delilah called the Philistines and told them what Samson had told her. They brought her the ropes and she tied Samson up. As soon as she was finished, she woke him up.

"Samson, wake up! The Philistines are here!"

And Samson stood up, breaking the thick ropes like they were made of paper.

"Where are the Philistines?" he asked, getting ready for a fight.

Delilah pouted. "They're not here. It was just a test to see if you told me the truth. Clearly, you don't trust me enough."

Samson felt bad about hurting Delilah, so the next night, he gave her a different answer.

"Looms are my real weakness," he said. "If you want to see me with my strength gone, braid my hair and weave it to your loom."

Delilah did this as Samson slept. Afterwards, she shouted, "Samson, wake up! The Philistines are here!"

Samson woke up, breaking the loom. His braid also came undone, his hair spilling over his shoulders.

Delilah cried. "Liar. I should have known you would never tell me the truth."

For days, Delilah did not speak to Samson. Samson gave her gifts to try to earn her forgiveness, but she remained angry.

Samson had no choice. "Please do not be mad at me. If you forgive me, I will tell you my true weakness."

But Delilah kept pouting. "And how am I supposed to believe you? You have lied to me so many times."

"Not this time," Samson said.

Delilah sighed. "Fine." Then she looked into his eyes. "Tell me."

"I have never once had a haircut," Samson told her. "And that is because my strength is in my hair."

Delilah looked at Samson's long hair, which she had always thought was unusually long. Why didn't she think that was where his strength lay?

"Do you forgive me?" Samson asked her.

She gave him a hug. "Yes. After all, now I know that you really love me."

"I do," Samson said. "So stop frowning."

Delilah smiled. It seemed that she would finally get her reward.

That night, Delilah stroked Samson's hair until he fell asleep, and after his eyelids had fallen shut, she set to work cutting every lock of hair on his head.

When Delilah was finished giving Samson his first ever haircut, she woke him up in the usual way.

"Samson, the Philistines are here!" she shouted.

Samson woke up, ready to fight as before, but he could barely stay on his feet. He just felt so...weak. The Philistines rushed inside the house and easily took him down, then they made him blind, tied him up in chains and dragged him away.

Word spread that Samson had been defeated, and the Philistines celebrated. As they prepared for a feast, Samson sat in prison.

"I am such a fool," he thought. "I shouldn't have trusted a woman again but I did not learn my lesson, and now, I cannot escape my fate."

Alone in the darkness, his hair grew, and his strength returned, but Samson did not let it show. He was saving all of it for a plan.

On the day of the feast of the Philistines, Samson was brought out of jail for the Philistines' entertainment. He could tell that a huge crowd of them had gathered. He could hear them eating and drinking and laughing at him.

"Look at the strongest Israelite now," they scoffed. "He is just as weak as the rest of them."

Samson did not listen to them. Instead, he prayed.

"Dear God, help me make things right. Lend me your strength one last time so that I may do what I was born to do."

God heard Samson's prayer and sent a boy to him.

"What do you need?" the boy asked him.

"Guide me to the biggest pillars," Samson said.

The boy did, and Samson placed his hands on the pillars.

"Now, leave," he told the boy. "For I will destroy this place."

The boy was confused. "But won't you get destroyed, too?"

"It's fine," Samson said, managing a weak smile. "I must pay for my mistake just as the Philistines will pay for their crimes."

The boy ran off. As soon as Samson could no longer hear the boy's footsteps, he gathered all of his strength. Groaning, he pushed against the pillars with all his might. They cracked and so did the arches holding the roof. With one last push, they fell, toppling the other pillars one by one. The Philistines screamed and tried to run away, but many of them were trapped under the fallen pillars and crushed under the pieces of the roof with Samson.

When Manoah heard what had happened to his son, he cried, but the Israelites rejoiced, knowing that thousands more of their enemies had been taken down. In their eyes, Samson was truly a hero.

An Old Man's Good News

A round the time of the birth of Jesus, roughly a thousand years after the reign of King David, many things had changed in Israel. It was now part of the Roman Empire, its rulers, including the reigning one, King Herod, chosen by Rome. As such, the Israelites followed Roman law. Many still worshiped the God of their ancestors, though, and they would come to the temples to pray. Some became priests who made offerings to God on behalf of the people.

Zacharias was one such priest, who lived with his wife, Elisabeth, a good woman who also followed the teachings of God. They loved each other very much, but sadly, they were not blessed with any children.

"If only I had a son, I would ask for nothing more," Elisabeth would often say with a sigh.

Zacharias would pat her shoulder and comfort her. "I do not know why God has decided not to give us any children until now, but whatever His reason, we must put our trust in Him, and we must not give up hope."

However, as the years passed and no child was born, Zacharias and Elisabeth began to lose heart. When Elisabeth passed the age where a woman could give birth, she finally gave up.

"It seems God has decided never to make me a mother," she said, trying to hold back her tears. "But why? I have done nothing but follow his commands."

Zacharias placed his arms around her. "Do not be sad. Like I said, God must have a good reason for not giving us a child. Maybe he has a better plan for us. Who are we to question His wisdom?"

More years passed. By now, Zacharias was an old man. His hair had turned white. His skin was covered in wrinkles. Every day, his back and his knees hurt, but he continued fulfilling his duties as a priest, one of which was to offer incense at the altar. When it was his turn, he took the incense and went inside the room of prayer. He was supposed to be alone, but when he got in, he saw someone else standing there - not even another priest but a stranger in glowing, white clothes.

Zacharias stumbled back, his eyes wide. "Who - who are you?"

"Do not be afraid, Zacharias," the stranger said. "Instead, be happy because God is about to grant you your heart's greatest desire. You and Elizabeth will have the son you have been waiting for, and you shall name him 'John', which means 'God is with him', for indeed, God will be with him all his life. He will walk before the Lord and open the hearts of the people to prepare them for his coming."

Zacharias stared at the stranger, who he knew now was a messenger of God. He had heard the messenger say that he and his wife would finally have children, but after that, he was so shocked that everything seemed muffled.

What did the messenger say? That his son would prepare a way for the Lord? What did that even mean?

"A-are you s-sure?" Zacharias stammered, his thoughts floating around in his head. "I am already old, and my wife cannot have children anymore. How do I know that - that everything you said will come true?"

"God is always sure about his plans," the messenger said. "And he asked me, his servant, Gabriel, to tell you this good news, but because you did not believe me, from now on, you will not be able to speak until everything I have just said comes true."

Then Gabriel left.

Zacharias opened his mouth to call Gabriel back and apologize, but no sound came out, not even a peep. His voice was gone.

Zacharias placed his hand on his throat. "So everything God's messenger said is true," he thought.

Then he slapped his forehead. Why did he have to act like such a fool and doubt God's word?

He offered the incense at the altar, then went down on his knees, closed his eyes, and prayed.

"Forgive me, dear God, for not believing Your messenger, and after he gave me such great news, too. I have made a mistake, and I accept my punishment. I will wait silently for the child You have promised, the proof of Your goodness and mercy."

Outside the room, the other priests started to mumble.

"Wasn't Zacharias just supposed to offer incense?" one of them asked. "What is taking him so long in there?"

"Should we go and check on him?" another wondered. "He is already old, after all. What if he tripped and got hurt?"

Just as another priest was about to check on Zacharias, he came out. The other priests sighed with relief.

"Zacharias, what were you doing in there? You got us all worried. Weren't you - ?"

They stopped talking as soon as they saw the look on his face, which clearly told them something had happened in the room.

"What happened?" they asked.

But Zacharias didn't answer. He just clasped his hands together and kept praying silently.

"God must have given him a vision," someone guessed. "So let us leave him alone for now."

Zacharias went home. As soon as Elisabeth saw him, she went to greet him.

"Welcome home, husband!" she said.

But Zacharias stayed silent.

Elisabeth's eyebrows bunched up. "What is wrong?" she asked. "What happened at the temple?"

Because Zacharias could not speak, he went inside the house and looked for something to write on. He wrote down everything that had happened - about his encounter with God's messenger at the temple, about the good news that they would finally be blessed with a child, and about how his speech was taken away as punishment because he did not believe it at first.

Elisabeth was also filled with disbelief. "Am I really going to be a mother at last?" she asked.

Zacharias nodded. He hugged her, and the two of them cried tears of joy.

Weeks later, Elisabeth got pregnant. She wanted to tell the whole world her good news, but she knew the people would be baffled, and she did not want to have to explain anything, so she hid inside the house. Only her servants and closest relatives who came to visit her, including her cousin, Mary, learned about her condition.

When Elisabeth gave birth, though, her news could no longer remain a secret. As the cries of a newborn baby boy filled the house, word spread around the neighborhood and around the town that Elisabeth and Zacharias now had a son.

"I can hardly believe it," a neighbor said. "Aren't Zacharias and Elisabeth too old to have children? Why, they are even older than my parents, and yet, I've heard that they now have a son."

"It's a miracle!" another neighbor exclaimed.

Elisabeth, of course, was the happiest woman in the world, her wish granted, and Zacharias was happy, too, but he was starting to worry.

"My son is born now," he thought. "And yet my voice still hasn't returned. Is God still angry with me?"

After eight days, it was time to name the baby. Many of Elisabeth and Zacharias' relatives came to the house, curious about what the baby would be called.

"Surely, the boy must be named Zacharias like his father," they said.

But Elisabeth shook her head. "I believe the child shall be called John."

Her relatives scratched their heads. "Why John? There is no one in our family named John."

"It is an unusual name," a few of them agreed.

"Why don't we ask Zacharias?" one of Zacharias' cousins suggested, thinking that Zacharias would want his only son named after him.

He stood before Zacharias, who was sitting quietly in a corner.

"What do you want to call your son?" he asked. "Do you want his name to be Zacharias, too?"

Zacharias stood up, looked for a writing tablet, and wrote, "His name is John."

Everyone became either confused or amazed. The child was really to be called a different name than his father's?

"Are you sure?" Zacharias' cousin asked.

Zacharias opened his mouth, and to his and everyone's surprise, his voice came out.

"His name is John."

As everyone gasped, not knowing what else to say, Elisabeth let out a breath of relief and smiled. Finally, her husband could speak again.

Zacharias took the baby from her arms and began praising God. "Blessed be the God of Israel who always looks after His people. He has fulfilled his promise to Abraham, to all the prophets, that we will be delivered from our enemies, so that from this day on, we need only trust in Him and fear nothing."

Then Zacharias kissed the top of his son's head and spoke to him.

"My dear boy, you will be known as a prophet of God, and you will prepare a way for the Lord. Those who hear you will turn away from their wicked ways, and those who live in darkness will find light and peace."

Hearing these words, everyone in the house became even more amazed.

"Surely, John will be great," they said.

Indeed, John grew up to become a prophet, preaching God's word to many, and later, Jesus would come to him to be baptized, making him known as John the Baptist.

King Herod Isn't Happy

When a king is born, there is usually a grand celebration throughout the whole kingdom. There are fireworks painting the sky, trumpets blaring, and music in the air. There are people cheering, young and old alike. When Jesus was born, all he had was a choir of angels and a star shining right above him up in the sky, but that star was even brighter than a firecracker, almost as bright as the moon, sending the whole of Bethlehem aglow in the darkness of the night. It was so bright it could even be seen in nearby countries.

In a country to the east, there were men who studied all sorts of things - numbers, languages, animals, plants, and even the stars. Because of this, they were called wise men. On the night Jesus was born, one wise man, Gaspar, was looking up at the sky, studying the stars. All of a sudden, a new star appeared.

"What is this?" he wondered excitedly. "I have never seen a new star being born before, and this one is very bright, too!"

He was very puzzled, so he woke up his friends, Melchior and Balthasar, who were also wise men. "What do you think this new star means?" he asked them.

They scratched their heads because they didn't know either.

Together, they looked through every scroll in the library until they found the answer. The bright new star was the king's star! This meant there was a new king!

"Judging by the location of the star, the new king must be in Israel," Gaspar said. "Let us go and see him."

"Let us worship this new King of the Jews and bring him gifts," Melchior agreed.

Balthasar nodded. "It will be a long journey, but let us go. It is not everyday we get to see a king's star, after all."

The three wise men packed their things and their gifts, loaded their camels, and made their way to Israel. They crossed sandy deserts, which were scorching hot during the day and freezing at night. Sometimes, a strong wind whipped the sand across their bodies and made it hard for them to see anything, but they kept going, following the star. They were afraid it might disappear just as suddenly as it had appeared, so they had to hurry.

Finally, they reached Israel. They headed to the palace in Judea where King Herod lived, thinking the new king would be there, too.

"We have come to honor the king," they said.

The guards led them to the throne room, where King Herod was happy to receive them and their gifts.

"Welcome, visitors," he told them. "I've heard you are wise men from a faraway land who have come just to see me. As such, I will treat you as my honored guests. Please make yourselves comfortable."

But the three wise men felt very uncomfortable. They looked at each other, frowning and scratching their heads.

"Is there something wrong?" King Herod asked them.

"We're afraid there has been some mistake," Gaspar said. "We have come to see the newborn king, the one with the new star."

"A new king?" King Herod scratched his head as well.

He had sons, but they were all no longer children. Who was this new king the wise men were talking about?

King Herod decided to gather his chief priests and the important officials of his court to find out if they knew.

"Tell me who this new king is," he ordered.

"You are our only king, Your Majesty," one of the officials answered.

"And yet, wise men have come from far away because they saw the king's star," King Herod said. "So there must be another king who was just born. Find out where he is."

The chief priests and officials got busy, going through their scrolls. Suddenly, one of them shouted, "I found something about a new king!"

"Give me that!" A court official grabbed the scroll and read it. "It says here that there will be a king to come from the town of Bethlehem, which does not make any sense. Why would a king come from such a small town?"

"Nevertheless, we should send some soldiers to find him," another official said. "Israel cannot have two kings."

"He is right," another said. "Let us bring the child here to the palace and get rid of him."

King Herod shook his head. "If we send soldiers and bring this child to the palace, everyone will know about him," he said. "If we are to get rid of this other king, this false king, we must do so quietly."

The chief priests and court officials nodded.

King Herod talked to the three wise men again.

"Good news!" he said with a big smile. "We have found out where this new king is. He is in Bethlehem."

"Very well," Gaspar said. "Then we shall be on our way to see him."

"Yes, please go and see him," King Herod urged. "Just promise me one thing."

"What is it?" Melchior asked.

"That you will come back afterwards and tell me exactly where this child is," King Herod answered. "So that I may send some gifts for him, too."

"Gladly," Balthasar answered.

King Herod nodded. "Now, go and have a safe journey. I will wait for your return."

Gaspar, Melchior, and Balthasar followed the star to Bethlehem. To their surprise, they found it shining right above a manger. Inside, they found a child sleeping in his mother's arms, surrounded by donkeys and sheep.

"Who are you?" Mary asked them, surprised.

"We are wise men from a faraway land who have come to worship the new king," the wise men answered, then they bowed before Mary. "Please accept our gifts."

Mary knew in her heart that they had been sent by God. "Thank you," she told them. "I know we do not have much to offer, but please stay and rest a while. If you've come so far, you must be tired."

That night, the three wise men slept near the manger. They slept peacefully because they were tired and they were happy that they had finally found the king they were looking for. Suddenly, though, just as suddenly as the new star had shown up in the sky, God whispered to them in their dreams.

"Do not return to King Herod," God told them. "For he is planning to harm the child you have found."

Gaspar woke up worried. "Oh no!" he said. "We should never have told King Herod about the newborn king."

Melchior, too, woke up and looked at his friend. "Did you just have a dream about King Herod's wicked plan?"

Balthasar yawned. "I did, too. I heard a voice saying we must not see King Herod again."

"Then we will not," Gaspar said. "It was a sign that led us here. Now, we must also follow another sign and leave here."

"If King Herod wanted to send gifts to the child, he could have given them to us," Melchior said. "So maybe he doesn't want to send any, after all."

"I do not know how three people can have the same dream," Balthasar said. "But I know something beyond our understanding is at work here. If so, we only have to play our part and do as we are told."

So the three wise men returned to their country in secret, passing by a different way than the one they first took.

That same night, God also had a message for Joseph, Mary's husband, in his dream.

"Wake up, Joseph!" God said. "Take Mary and Jesus and go to Egypt, and do not come back until I tell you to, for the child's life is in danger."

Joseph got up and shook Mary gently. "Wake up, Mary."

Mary rubbed her eyes. "What's wrong, Joseph?"

"God has sent me a message," Joseph said. "Jesus is in danger, so we must leave at once."

Hearing this, Mary immediately got up and changed her clothes. They gathered their things, wrapped baby Jesus warmly, and started on their journey to Egypt.

The days passed. Each day, King Herod waited for the wise men to return so he could find the newborn king, but there was no sign of them. Finally, King Herod got tired of waiting.

"They tricked me!" he shouted angrily. "They are not coming back! I gave them a warm welcome and this is what they do to me? They made a promise to me, and they broke it! How dare they?"

"Your Majesty, should we have them hunted down?" a royal adviser asked.

King Herod took a deep breath as he tried to calm down. "As much as I want to punish the wise men, they are not my subjects. Besides, what is more important is the child. I cannot let a threat to my throne live."

"Then shall we send the army to take care of the child now?" another adviser asked.

"But we do not know where exactly this child is," another pointed out.

King Herod clenched his fists. "Send the army to Bethlehem," he ordered. "And tell the soldiers to get rid of every child born in the past two years, male or female, not just in Bethlehem but in the surrounding towns. This way, I can be sure that the throne remains mine. Only mine."

King Herod's army marched to Bethlehem and did as he commanded. Many babies and young children were lost, all because of one king's greed, but the baby Jesus survived, already on his way to Egypt with Mary and Joseph, and they would live there until the end of King Herod's reign.

Jesus Goes To A Wedding

When Jesus was about thirty years old, he went to his cousin, John, to be baptized in the Jordan River. Afterwards, he went home to find his mother, Mary, packing some bags.

"Are you traveling somewhere, Mother?" Jesus asked.

"Oh, you're back." Mary gave her son a hug. "I was just going to Cana where one of our relatives is getting married. I'm sure they need all the help they can get with the wedding feast."

Jesus smiled. He remembered a story his father once told him about how his mother, while pregnant with him, traveled far and all by herself just to visit John's mother, who she had learned was also pregnant at the time. His mother always put others first, which was why it was no wonder God was with her. It was also one of the things Jesus admired about her.

"Why don't you come along?" Mary asked Jesus. "Our relatives will be happy to see you. You can bring your new friends, too."

Jesus did get new friends recently - his disciples. They were ordinary men, mostly fishermen, who he called to help him teach everyone about the kingdom of God. Some of them did not know each other very well yet, so Jesus thought it would be a good idea to spend time together at the wedding.

"We will be there," Jesus said.

The wedding feast started three days later. Mary, Jesus, his disciples and dozens of other people were present. As the newlywed couple celebrated with their guests, the servants were busy working in the kitchen.

They washed and chopped the fruits and vegetables. They grilled the fish and the meat. They kneaded the dough and baked the bread. They had to work continuously because there were many mouths to be fed.

"We cannot let our masters down, so we must keep the wine and food flowing," the head servant said. "Besides, if the guests are happy, the newlyweds will also be happy."

"They make such a good couple," a younger servant said as she took the freshly baked bread out of the oven. "I hope God will bless them with many children."

"Maybe we can ask one of the guests to pray for them," another said as she washed a plate. "I've heard that one of the guests is a man of God."

"Really?" Another servant raised his eyebrows as he looked up from the meat he was cooking. "Does he perform miracles? It would be nice if he made gold and silver rain from the sky or send down lightning to strike down those smug Roman soldiers."

"Or maybe fill all our pots with food that won't run out so we won't have to keep cooking?" the other servant suggested.

"Enough talk," the head servant scolded them. "We have plenty of work that needs doing."

The servants fell silent, and the kitchen was filled with only the symphony of knives, boiling water, sizzling meat, and roaring flames. After a while, though, a young boy rushed in, breathing rapidly and looking like he was being chased by a pack of wolves.

"What's the matter with you, boy?" the head servant asked.

"My father says there is no more wine!" the boy shouted in a panic.

The head servant's eyes grew wide, then he ran out of the kitchen. He ran to the cellar and saw only one barrel of wine left.

"Oh, dear! What shall we do?" He slapped his forehead. "This is a big problem! We cannot have a wedding feast without wine. I will go and tell the master."

At that time, the master was speaking with Mary.

"Thank you for coming and even helping with the feast," he told her. "Preparing a wedding feast is not easy, but with friends and relatives to help, it becomes easier as well as a much more joyous occasion."

"You are welcome," Mary said. "I am just glad I was able to help even a little."

"You were," he told her. "So now, please enjoy the feast with your son. He has grown into such a fine man."

"He has," Mary agreed, looking over at Jesus with pride and love in her eyes.

Just then, the head servant appeared. "Master, I'm afraid we have a problem," he said in a worried tone.

The master became concerned but tried to keep a straight face. "What is the problem?"

"There is no more wine," the head servant told him.

"What do you mean?" The master could not hide his worry any longer. "Didn't we buy several barrels?"

"Yes, but there is only one left, so the wine will soon run out," the head servant answered.

The master touched his chin. "Well, we do have a lot of guests." Then he scratched his head. "Still, I didn't think the wine would run out. If it does, our guests will have nothing to drink."

"Maybe we can ask if our neighbors have wine?" the head servant suggested.

The master shook his head. "There is no way we'd have enough."

"But the vineyard is too far away," the head servant said. "If we sent someone to buy wine, it would take days before they came back. The wedding feast will be over by then."

"I know." The master's forehead wrinkled. "Just as I know that there can be no feast without wine. And our most important guests are still here, too. But what should I do? What can I do? It will take a miracle to solve this problem."

Mary had been listening to them talk, and she had grown concerned, so she spoke.

"Is there anything else you want my help with?" she asked.

The master forced a smile. "No. You have done enough. Please enjoy the feast. I will figure something out. God is merciful, after all."

Then he left with his head servant.

Mary knew, however, that her relative was deeply troubled, and she could not just leave him alone. Maybe there was nothing she could do to help, but she knew someone who could definitely do something.

She went to Jesus and sat beside him. "Son, they have a problem," she whispered in his ear. "There is no more wine."

Jesus looked at her. "What do you want me to do, Mother?"

Mary said nothing.

Jesus sighed. "Well, whatever you want me to do, now is not yet the time."

Mary nodded. She left her son's side, but she knew him better than anyone, so she knew he would not be able to turn her down. She went to the cellar and spoke to the master and the servants there.

"If my son tells you to do anything, whatever it is, just do it without asking any questions," she said.

Then she left, leaving the master and the servants puzzled.

"Whatever does she mean?" the master asked as he scratched the back of his neck.

The other servants only shrugged.

Moments later, Jesus went into the cellar. A few of his disciples followed him, curious about what he would do.

"Is it true that the wine is running out?" Jesus asked.

The master nodded. "Sadly. And since there is no way for me to get more, I will just have to ask the guests to leave, even those from the governor's house."

Jesus checked the barrels and found them empty indeed. Then he went to the kitchen, looking around.

"Is he Mary's son?" one of the servants asked one of Jesus' disciples curiously.

"Yes," the disciple answered.

"What is he looking for?" another servant asked. "What is he planning?"

The disciple shrugged. "All I know is that Jesus is someone loved by God. We can only wait and see."

So they watched and waited. Finally, Jesus spoke again.

"Fill these with water from the well," he said, pointing to the stone pots in a corner.

The servants looked confused. What was the point of filling up pots with water when it was wine that was running out? Were they just going to serve the guests water now?

"If we serve the guests water instead of wine, they will leave," the head servant reminded his master.

But the master remembered what Mary had said. "Go and do as he said," he ordered.

The servants obeyed, carrying the pots and filling them with water from the well.

When they returned, Jesus told them, "Now, fill the cups of the guests, starting with the most important ones."

The servants looked even more confused, and even the master of the house hesitated.

"I cannot serve water to my guests," he thought.

But what else could he do? He did not have any more wine. Surely, water was better than nothing at all.

Sighing, the master nodded his head. "Go serve our guests," he ordered.

The servants looked at each other and at the oldest servant, thinking that the master must have lost his mind. Even the head servant did not know what his master was thinking or what Jesus was planning, but he had no choice but to make sure the orders were carried out.

"The master has given an order," he told them, clapping his hands. "So get moving and follow them."

The servants went out and started pouring the water from the pots into the cups of the guests, starting with the cup of the guest from the governor's house. As the important guest drank, the master and the servants held their breath. Then they got worried as the guest called the master over.

"What is wrong with you?" the guest asked.

The master swallowed the lump in his throat. "I am sorry, but..."

"Why did you wait until now to serve the best wine?" the guest continued. "Shouldn't you have served that first? I was about to leave, too."

The master's eyes grew wide. Quickly, he grabbed a cup and asked a servant to pour him water, which he gulped down quickly. Afterwards, he laughed.

"This is truly wine!" he said. "And the best wine I've ever tasted!"

The other guests agreed, even the disciples.

"How can this be?" they wondered. "Didn't we see the servants draw water from the well?"

"It's a miracle!" they said. "Jesus is truly someone sent by God!"

Jesus, however, said nothing. His mother, too, only smiled. They were the only ones who knew what had just happened, just as they knew that it would only be the first of many miracles to come.

Food For Everyone

As his friends, Jesus' disciples accompanied him everywhere. They grew to care for him, so when they heard some horrible news, they had a hard time telling him.

"What is it?" Jesus asked, noticing their anxiety.

"Your cousin, John, is gone," they told Jesus sadly. "We heard he was executed on King Herod's orders."

A few days before, during a feast at the royal palace, King Herod was so happy with his new stepdaughter's dance that he promised to give her anything, and she just happened to ask for the head of John the Baptist because she knew her mother, the new queen, did not like him. King Herod had planned on leaving John alone, afraid that he was like one of the powerful prophets of old who could summon fire from the sky, but he had given the girl his word, and everyone at court had heard it. He had no choice but to fulfill his promise, and the girl got her wish.

Jesus' heart sank as he heard this news, not just because John was his cousin who he thought of as a brother, but because John was also a man of God. All he ever did was good, and all he ever spoke was the truth, yet he lost his life because of a woman's cruelty.

"Let us go to a place where no one will find us," he told his disciples. "Somewhere quiet so I can grieve for my cousin."

His disciples understood. "We have decided to stay by your side, Lord, so we will go wherever you go."

Jesus and his disciples tried to leave town without anyone knowing, but news always has a way of traveling around. A fisherman heard one of the disciples trying to borrow a boat.

"Jesus is going somewhere," he said to his friend, who was a carpenter. "Who knows where he will go next?"

Later, that carpenter spoke to his wife. "It seems Jesus is leaving town tomorrow. Didn't you say you wanted to see him?"

"I did," the carpenter's wife admitted. "I've heard he can perform miracles. Also, it seems he is very good at speaking. Everyone who hears him speak is convinced that his words come straight from the mouth of God."

"Well, you've lost your chance to see him or hear him speak," the carpenter said. "Or do you plan on following him out of town?"

The carpenter's wife had not planned on that, but her husband had given her an idea, one she shared with her friend, a farmer's wife.

"Didn't you tell me one of your sons gets sick a lot?" she said. "Why don't we go bring him to Jesus? I hear he is going out of town. If we follow him, we can ask him to cure your son."

"But we don't even know where Jesus is going," the farmer's wife said.

The carpenter's wife shrugged. "Does that matter? We will just have to bring some food with us. I will cook some fish, and you can bake some bread, and we will put them all in a basket."

The farmer's wife nodded. "Very well."

"Oh, and one last thing," the farmer's wife said. "Do not tell anyone what I told you about Jesus leaving. It will be our secret."

Still, other people heard about Jesus leaving and like the two women, they followed Jesus across the lake and into the mountains, forming a huge crowd.

When the disciples saw the crowd, they became worried.

"Maybe we should tell them to go away and leave Jesus alone," some of them said.

Peter was concerned as well, so he decided to talk to Jesus.

"Jesus, we know you wanted to be alone," Peter said. "But there are many people who have followed us here. Shall we tell them to go away?"

"How many?" Jesus asked.

Peter scratched the back of his head as he tried to think. "Maybe thousands?"

Jesus went with Peter to look at the crowd. Sure enough, there were so many of them sitting all over the place, some on the grass, some on rocks and some under the trees. Many of them were poor, their clothes with holes in some places. There were some sick people, too, and some children and old people.

Seeing them, Jesus felt a tug on his heart. These people reminded him of children without a mother or father, of animals without a master, of sheep without a shepherd.

"Leave them alone," Jesus said. "I will speak with them and heal those who are sick."

The disciples gathered the crowds and asked them to bring the sick people to the front. Jesus placed his hands on them, and they were immediately healed of all their sicknesses. Afterwards, he sat and began to preach God's word.

"If you want to have something, ask for it," Jesus told them. "If you are missing something, search for it. If you see a closed door in front of you, knock, and it will be opened."

He also taught them not to be blinded by money.

"If you think you can love both God and money, you are wrong. You must choose one, and why choose money when it can be lost or stolen? Even if you become the richest man on earth, will you be happy? Choose God instead, and you will never have to worry about what you will eat or drink or wear tomorrow. Each day comes with its own problems, but if you put God first, everything else will be given to you."

The people listened in amazement, glad that they had followed Jesus. They were a little tired from walking so far but not anymore. They just felt blessed.

The hours went by. As the sun began to sink, the disciples started worrying.

"Soon, it will be dark," one of them said. "Shouldn't we tell Jesus to send these people home?"

Philip, a disciple, went to Jesus. "Lord," he said. "Send the people away so that they can go to the villages and buy themselves food before it gets too late."

Jesus looked at the people, noticing that some of them were indeed already hungry, touching their bellies. He told Philip, "Why don't you go to the nearest village and get them all something to eat?"

Philip's eyes grew wide, then he looked at the crowd. He was sure there were thousands of people there.

"Lord, I know you would like to feed everyone, and so do I, but we do not have enough money," he said to Jesus. "We can only buy a few loaves of bread at most."

Jesus nodded. "And how much food do the people have?"

Philip looked at them once more. "Many of them have none," he said.

Andrew, the brother of Peter, spoke. "Lord, there is a boy who has a basket of food - five loaves of bread and two pieces of fish. That is the most anyone has."

Jesus looked at Andrew. "Bring the food to me."

Andrew brought the boy carrying the basket of food to Jesus. The boy seemed scared to be near someone so important, but Jesus smiled at him.

"Come closer," Jesus said to the boy. "And don't be afraid."

The boy took a step forward. "Are you taking our food?" he asked shyly.

Jesus patted the boy's head. "Don't worry. I will make sure everyone has food to eat."

Then he turned to his disciples. "Tell everyone to group themselves into fifty and sit comfortably on the grass," he ordered.

The disciples were puzzled.

"Are we really feeding everyone?" they asked one another. "With just five loaves and two fish?"

"What? Are we going to toss them crumbs?" one complained. "But that will turn them into a mob, and then, we'll be in trouble."

"Surely, Jesus has something planned," Peter told them. "So let us just do what he told us to do."

As they told the people to sit down, Jesus took the basket of food in his hands and lifted his eyes to heaven, praying. Then when the disciples came back, Jesus broke the bread and cut the fishes into pieces, and told the disciples to put them inside the other baskets and give them to the people - one for each group.

The disciples obeyed, though they were worried still.

When Philip gave one of the baskets to a group of fifty people, he felt ashamed. "I am sorry, but this is all we have," he said.

He waited to hear them grumbling, but to his surprise, they just took the food and ate.

Everyone else was doing the same, gobbling up all the bread and fish as if they were eating grilled goat meat and pies. Philip felt confused. Shouldn't they have ran out of food by now?

Peter tapped his shoulder and gave him some food. "Eat," he said. "You must be hungry, too."

Philip had to admit that he was also hungry, so he ate, and he could not believe how delicious the food was.

All around the camp, people were also enjoying every bite, and when they were done, they smiled as they rubbed their bellies.

"I am so full I feel like I've just eaten a horse," the carpenter's wife said.

"But where did all this food come from?" the farmer's wife wondered. She looked at the boy sitting beside her. "Didn't you just give Jesus a bit of fish and a few loaves?"

The boy nodded.

The carpenter's wife looked inside the basket. "But there are still even more loaves of bread and fish here."

Then her eyes grew wide. "It must be a miracle!" she exclaimed. "Jesus has multiplied the food!"

The people began to murmur among themselves, and realizing what had happened, praised God.

"Jesus is indeed the Son of God!" some said. "Let us make him our king."

"That is a good idea," the others agreed. "If Jesus was our king, we would never go hungry."

However, Jesus knew what the people were thinking, and he snuck out to be alone.

The Wind And The Waves

After leaving the crowds, Jesus told his disciples, "I will go pray on the mountain, so go ahead across the sea, and I will meet you on the other side."

"Yes, Lord," they replied.

The disciples boarded the boat to cross the sea, and soon, it set sail.

At first, the weather was perfectly fine. The only specks of white on the blue sky were the wings of the birds that flew. There were hardly any folds on the surface of the sea, hardly any waves rising and falling. The wind was a cool whisper, brushing against the sails and tickling the cheeks of everyone on deck.

As the breeze blew, one of the disciples, James, smiled. "This feels so refreshing, especially when we've been working so hard these past few days."

"It is," another disciple, the one named Andrew, agreed. "I did not realize just how hard being a disciple would be or how much we would walk, so I am glad to be on a boat again on a lovely day like this."

Peter, Andrew's brother and the leader of the disciples, however, did not look too happy. "I wish Jesus was here. Is it really okay to leave him alone? What if the people find him and take him away?"

"Jesus will be fine," Andrew assured his brother. "He is the Son of God, remember? I'm sure he will be with us again before we know it, so for now, just enjoy this boat trip, brother."

Peter tried, and he did end up enjoying the trip, but what he did not know was that the wind and the waves sometimes get minds of their own.

"We have been behaving all day," said the waves. "Now, it's time for us to have some fun, and that big boat looks like the perfect toy."

"I am done being quiet and gentle," said the wind. "Now, I will blow as hard as I can and make as much noise as I want."

Dark clouds rolled in to block the blue sky. The wind began to howl. The waves rose and rocked the boat.

As they got wet, the passengers on board the boat started to panic.

"The boat is going to sink!" they cried. "The sea will swallow us all up, and we will drown."

"Please, God, save us!" some of them prayed.

The disciples were scared, too.

"Why did this have to happen when Jesus isn't here?" James complained. "If Jesus were here, he could easily part the sea like Moses once did."

"And what good would that do?" John, his brother, who was also a disciple, asked. "Do you want to walk across the sea? I thought you said you were tired of walking."

Andrew turned to his own brother. "We will be fine, right? Even if Jesus isn't here, Jesus would not let any-thing bad happen to us."

"Of course," Peter said, trying to sound confident. "We are Jesus' disciples and friends, and he is the Son of God. That means we are special in God's eyes. He will never abandon us."

The truth was that Peter was also scared, but part of being the leader of the disciples meant not showing any fear, especially when everyone else was already afraid. Besides, he wanted to believe that Jesus would come and save them.

"Dear God," he prayed. "I know you can see us in this boat and that you can hear my prayer. Please save us. Show us your goodness and mercy."

Suddenly, someone screamed. "There is a...a...g-g-ghost on the water!"

Peter opened his eyes and looked. Sure enough, there was a figure dressed in white floating on the water, seemingly not caring about the wind or the waves.

"It has come for us!" a passenger cried out in fear. "It is going to take our souls and put us on a different boat to the afterlife."

Peter didn't say anything. He didn't have any words for his jumbled thoughts that were being drowned by all the noise around him. He only knew it did not make any sense for a ghost to appear, especially in the middle of the sea. But if it was not a ghost, what was this floating figure?

"Do not be afraid, Peter," a voice suddenly said. "It is me, Jesus."

Peter squinted as he tried to get a closer look at the figure. Was it really Jesus? He couldn't see clearly with the wind and the seawater in his face.

"Are you really the Lord Jesus?" Peter asked. "If you are, let me take a closer look at you so I can see your face."

"Go ahead and look," Jesus invited him. "Get out of the boat and come to me."

Peter stood up and walked to the edge of the ship. The boat was rocking and his knees were shaking, so he fell a few times, but eventually, he made it.

"Peter, what are you doing?" the other disciples asked him. "You'll fall over."

"He must have gone mad," the passengers thought.

But Peter kept going. Seeing the waves, he was filled with fear, but he closed his eyes, gathered his courage, and jumped.

He thought he would hear a splash, but to his surprise, there was none. The sea stayed right beneath his sandals. He was standing on water!

"Come to me," Jesus called Peter again.

Peter knew now that it must really be Jesus calling to him, and he kept his eyes on the white figure in front of him as he put one foot in front of the other, walking on water.

The disciples and the other people on the boat realized what was happening, and they were both amazed and afraid.

"Is that really Peter walking on water or am I dreaming?" James asked, rubbing his eyes.

"It is Peter," Andrew said. "He is performing a miracle."

Peter could hardly believe it, too, but he just kept going. He had forgotten all about the wind and the waves.

Of course, the wind and the waves did not like this.

"No one is supposed to walk all over me," the waves said. "Let us move even faster and stand taller."

"I will blow right in his ear so he won't ignore me," the wind said.

When Peter heard the wind in his ear, he looked down. He saw the waves crashing at his feet and he went still, fear creeping into his heart.

"What am I doing in the middle of the sea?" he asked himself. Then he turned his head. "Is that the boat? I should go back."

As fear weighed on his heart, his feet began to sink into the sea. In seconds, the water reached to his ankles then to his knees, eventually swallowing him up to the waist. When the water had reached his chest, Peter tried to swim, but the waves were just too strong.

"We've got him now!" the wind and the waves cheered.

Jesus, on the other hand, still stood on the water. Peter called out to him. "Lord, I am drowning. Save me!"

Jesus walked towards Peter and grabbed his hand.

"You were doing something incredible just a few moments ago," Jesus told him. "Why did you stop believing?"

Then he pulled Peter out of the water and carried him back to the boat. When he was on deck, he looked at the waves and the wind. Just one look was enough to make them both behave again, and the weather went back to how it was, the dark clouds scurrying off.

The disciples and the other passengers were all in awe.

"Who is this man?" they wondered. "For truly, he is a man of God."

"He is the Son of God," John said. "And nothing is beyond his power."

That was not the only time Jesus showed his power over the wind and the waves. Another time, Jesus was on a boat again with his disciples. As he stood on the deck, the wind and the waves behaved, but after he took a nap, they started to cause trouble.

"Now is our chance," the waves said. "We can play around as much as we like."

"Now that Jesus is asleep, the people on the boat look so scared," the wind said. "Maybe I will scare them even more."

The waves rose and crashed against the sides of the boat. The wind whipped the sails. The rain joined in, too, and started pouring.

Throughout all this, Jesus stayed asleep.

"How can he sleep through a storm?" one of the disciples asked. "Can he not feel the rain or hear the wind?"

"Shouldn't we wake him up?" another asked, looking at Peter.

Peter looked at Jesus who was indeed sleeping soundly. He did not want to wake up his master, knowing Jesus was tired, but he was starting to get scared. What if the boat crashed?

Gently, he shook Jesus. "Lord, wake up. There is a storm and our boat might not make it through."

But Jesus did not open his eyes.

"Jesus, wake up!" the other disciples cried. "We need you!"

Jesus opened his eyes and saw the storm, but he was more concerned about the fear on Peter's face. He sat up and saw that the other disciples were also shaking.

"Why are you all so scared?" he asked them. "Did I not tell you that if you have even just a little bit of faith, you can move mountains?"

Then Jesus stood up and talked to the wind.

"Be quiet!" he ordered.

The wind immediately went into hiding.

Afterwards, he looked down at the waves.

"Stop moving!" he commanded.

At once, the waves went away. The water became still. Even the rain had stopped.

Again, Peter and the disciples knelt down before Jesus, bowing their heads. They felt like fools, worrying about the storm that Jesus sent away with just a few words.

As Jesus went back to sleep, Peter looked at the other disciples and whispered, "Let us have faith, for surely, if Jesus is with us, who even the wind and the waves listen to, nothing bad will happen to us."

The others nodded their heads. If even the wind and the waves obeyed Jesus, who were they to disobey him?

Where Are The Other Nine?

T hroughout his travels as he preached God's word, Jesus cured many sick people. He made men who had been born blind see and people who could no longer move their legs stand up from their mats and walk. He only had to touch them and say the word, and the sick would be healed, praising God.

One of the most common illnesses at the time, which did not have a cure was leprosy. Those who had leprosy, who were called lepers, had their skin covered in red or white sores and patches, so wherever they went, the other people stayed away in disgust.

"How horrible!" they would say as they tried not to look at the ugly sores. "They must have done something bad to be punished this way."

"Don't come near me!" they would shout whenever a leper passed by. "We don't want to catch your sickness and end up looking like you!"

Indeed, the lepers were often treated like monsters, so they stayed on the outskirts of town, away from most of the people.

In a small village along the road to Jerusalem, there lived ten lepers, and when they heard that Jesus was coming, they were excited.

"Maybe Jesus will heal us," one of them said. "I've heard he can perform miracles."

"Surely, he will take pity on us," another agreed. "No one will even look at us because of our sickness."

"But how will we get close to him?" another asked, worrying. "Surely, he will be surrounded by his disciples and many people who want to see him."

The others fell silent as they tried to think, then one of the lepers said, "Maybe we do not have to get close to him. If Jesus is as powerful as they say, maybe as long as he sees us, we can be healed."

"But how will we make him see us?" another leper asked.

"We have our voices, don't we?" the other leper answered. "When Jesus passes by, let us call out to him as loudly as we can."

Since none of the other lepers had a better idea, they decided to go along with the plan.

When Jesus passed by, the ten lepers shouted at the top of their lungs, "Jesus, have mercy on us!"

At first, Jesus did not hear them because there were many people trying to get his attention, so they shouted even louder, joining their hands around their mouths like a horn to make their voices reach farther.

"Jesus, have mercy on us!"

Jesus turned his head, and when he saw the lepers who were staying away from the crowd, his heart was indeed moved with pity, and he walked towards them.

"Lord, you must not go near the lepers," some of the people said. "Your clothes will get dirty with the blood coming out of their sores, and the smell will go on you."

However, Jesus did not listen to the people. He stood in front of the lepers and touched each one of them. Then he told them, "Go to the temple."

He told them this so that the priests would see them, but they did not understand.

"Why ask us to go to the temple?" they whispered among themselves. "Why not just cure us right now?"

"We're not allowed to go to the temple," some pointed out. "If we go there, the priests will just drive us out."

"But if it's Jesus who said so, then we should obey," one of them said. "For surely, he must have a reason."

The others were still not sure they wanted to go to the temple, but in the end, all of them did.

The lepers walked to the temple, doing their best to keep themselves hidden along the way, but one of them bumped into a child.

"I'm sorry," the leper quickly said, stepping away.

To his surprise, the child chuckled. "Why do you look so scared? And why are you all covered up on a hot day? You are so strange."

After the child left, the leper was puzzled. Why wasn't the child scared of him? Didn't he look like a monster?

Then he looked at his arms, and he could not believe his eyes. His sores were gone!

"I'm cured!" he said to the other lepers. "My sores are all gone!"

"They are!" one of them exclaimed. Then he looked at his own arms and found that his sores were gone, too. "My leprosy is gone!"

One by one, the lepers inspected themselves and found that their sores had disappeared as if they had been blown away by the wind. Their arms, their legs, their faces - all looked perfectly fine!

"We have been cured!" one of the lepers shouted, jumping up and down.

"It is a miracle!" another cheered.

"I thought I would never see my family again, but now I can," one of the lepers said with tears in his eyes. "I cannot wait to go back to them."

And he ran off. A few others did the same, while some ran to the temple, and some just began to run around, spreading the word that they had been cured.

Only one of the lepers who had been cured went back the way they came, thinking of looking for Jesus again.

"I must thank Jesus," he thought.

He ran back, and as soon as he saw Jesus, he knelt before him. "Thank you, Lord, for healing me! God, who works wonders through you, is truly good and merciful!"

Jesus was glad to see the leper he had cured, but he was also confused. He looked around and asked, "Weren't there ten of you that I healed? Where are the other nine? Is it only one who came back to give praise and thanks to God?"

The man in front of him no longer knew where his former companions were, so he said, "I'm sorry, Lord. I should have brought everyone back with me."

Jesus looked at him and patted his shoulder. "It's alright. Go home. Your faith has cured you."

The man stood up and left, praising God.

The people who had seen him were all amazed, but the disciples knew that there were also people who were starting to fear Jesus because of his power.

Once, after preaching at the temple in Jerusalem, some people threw stones at him.

"Maybe we should be more careful," they told Jesus.

But Jesus told them, "Whoever wants to save his own life will lose it, and whoever loses his life will save it."

The Man Who Came Back To Life

I n a town called Bethany, there was a man named Lazarus who lived with his two sisters, Martha and Mary. They were all friends of Jesus, having welcomed Jesus into their home before when he needed a place to rest with his disciples.

One evening, during dinner, Martha noticed that her brother wasn't eating or speaking much.

"Are you alright?" she asked.

Lazarus touched his head. "I think I'm coming down with something, but I'll be fine. You don't have to worry about me."

Martha frowned. "How can I not worry about my brother?"

"Remember what Jesus said," Mary told her. "Instead of worrying all the time, trust in God's goodness."

Martha did try not to worry, but the next day, Lazarus got sick, and he stayed in bed for days, getting worse and worse. The sisters called for a doctor, but even the doctor could not do much.

"Should we call for Jesus now?" Martha asked Mary.

By now, even Mary was worried, so she nodded. "Let us send a messenger to Jesus and tell him that Lazarus is very sick. Surely, he will come."

Jesus was with his disciples when the messenger from Bethany arrived.

"Lord, my master, Lazarus is very sick and has not been out of bed for days," the messenger said. "His sisters are worried that he might not get better."

Jesus frowned. He was fond of the three siblings, who had been nothing but good to him, and a part of him did want to rush to Bethany, but he took a deep breath.

"Thank you for telling me," he told the messenger.

After the messenger left, Peter spoke to Jesus. "I know that Judea is a bit dangerous right now, but don't you want to go to Bethany to see your friend, Lazarus? What if he doesn't recover from this sickness?"

Jesus looked at Peter. "Lazarus will live," he said. "And the glory of God will be revealed through His Son."

Peter did not understand what Jesus meant by that last part, but he said no more, trusting that Jesus knew what to do best.

For two more days, Jesus and his disciples stayed in the town where they were, then on the third day, Jesus said to them, "Let us go to Bethany."

Peter nodded, but the other disciples were worried.

"Lord, the last time we were in the province of Judea, the people tried to hurt you," one of the disciples reminded Jesus. "Are you sure we should go back there so soon?"

"We shall pass through that town during the night, then we will not be seen," Jesus said. "And we will make our way to Bethany where my friend, Lazarus, sleeps. It is time for me to get him out of his bed."

"If he is sleeping, doesn't that mean he will get better?" another disciple asked. "Why do we need to go see him?"

Jesus sighed and decided to tell his disciples the truth clearly. "Lazarus is gone."

The disciples gasped.

"I did not go to him before," Jesus continued. "But now, let us go, that you may truly believe in the glory of God."

The disciples did not understand these words.

"Why are we going to Bethany if Lazarus is already gone?" they wondered. "Won't Martha and Mary just be angry that Jesus did not do anything to keep their brother alive?"

One of the disciples, Thomas, spoke up. "I do not know what Jesus is planning, but we are his disciples, so let us just go with him. Whatever dangers or troubles await us, let us all face them together."

In Bethany, many people came to mourn Lazarus' passing. Of course, Martha and Mary grieved most of all, finding it hard to believe that the brother they loved was now gone.

Mary stayed mostly inside the house, crying and praying, but Martha had even more things to do now that Lazarus was gone. On the fourth day, while Martha was in town doing her errands, she heard people talking about Jesus.

"Have you heard?" they said. "That prophet, Jesus, is in the next town. Maybe he will mourn Lazarus also."

As soon as Martha heard this, she ran to the next town looking for Jesus. When she found him, she knelt before him, sobbing.

"Lord, why did you not come sooner?" she asked as tears streamed down her face. "If you had only been here, I'm sure Lazarus would still be here. Even so, I know that even now, you can do something, for God will surely grant whatever you wish for."

Jesus helped Martha stand up. "Do not weep," he told her. "For your brother will live again."

But Martha did not understand what Jesus meant. "I know that Lazarus will rise again when the day of the resurrection that you told us about comes," she said. "But I am still sad that he is gone."

"I am the resurrection and the life," Jesus told her. "Whoever believes in me will live forever. Do you believe this?"

Martha nodded. "I believe you can do all things, Lord, because you are the Son of God who He sent into this world."

Jesus patted her head. "Then go, tell your sister I have come."

Martha went back home, going straight to Mary's room.

"Mary, Jesus has arrived," she told her sister.

Mary, who had been crying on her knees, stood up. "Jesus is here?"

"He is in the next town," Martha said. "And he is calling for you."

Mary ran out of the house with Martha to go to Jesus. Some of the mourners saw them.

"Where are the sisters going?" they wondered.

"To Lazarus' tomb maybe," someone answered. "They must miss him dearly."

"Let us go with them then and comfort them," the other people said, and they started to follow Mary and Martha.

Lazarus' sisters went to where Jesus was staying. As soon as Mary saw Jesus, she, too, threw herself at his feet and started crying.

"Lord, if you had only been here, my brother would still be alive," she said between tears.

Jesus said nothing, not wanting to see Mary crying, and when he saw the people who had followed Mary, he felt even more troubled, and he frowned.

He grabbed Mary's arms and helped her stand so he could talk to her. "Where is your brother buried?" he asked.

Mary wiped her tears. "Come, Lord. I will show you."

Mary brought Jesus to the graveyard, the crowd of mourners and Jesus' disciples behind them. When they got there, Mary started to cry once more, and Jesus mourned with her.

"He must have loved Lazarus," the people whispered.

"But if so, why didn't he come sooner?" others asked. "He has healed many sick people, hasn't he? He has even made blind men see. Why couldn't he have healed his friend? Then Lazarus would have recovered and lived."

Jesus heard them, and he stood before Lazarus' tomb which was in a cave with a huge stone for a door.

"Roll away the stone," he ordered.

Martha stepped forward. "Lord, it has been four days. My brother's corpse will have a bad smell by now, and if we roll away the stone, everyone here will smell it."

Jesus looked at her, frowning. "I thought you said you believed in me. Do you not want to see the glory of God?"

Martha stepped back and gave the men orders to roll the stone away. As soon as it was out of the way, Jesus looked up and prayed.

"Father, thank You for hearing my prayer as always. I know You are always watching over me, and I hope that the people here will believe it, too, and believe that You have sent me."

Then Jesus looked at the entrance to the cave where Lazarus was buried.

"Come out, Lazarus!" he ordered.

At first, nothing happened, and everyone was silent as they held their breaths, then as someone wrapped in bandages came out of the cave, they gasped.

Lazarus had come back to life!

He had trouble walking, though, with all his bandages, so Jesus asked the others to help him. Mary and Martha did so, hugging him afterwards.

"We thought you were gone!" they said.

"I thought I was, too," he answered. Then he looked at Jesus and smiled. "But I believed you would come and save me."

The disciples went down on their knees, knowing that they had just seen another miracle, maybe the greatest one yet. The people, too, were amazed, and some of them ran off, spreading the word that Jesus had brought someone back to life.

Many of those who heard what had happened rejoiced and believed in Jesus, but the chief priests and the elders at the temple were not happy.

"At this rate, the people will make him king," they said. "Then the Romans will come and punish us all."

"Then maybe we should get rid of him first," the high priest, Caiaphas, said.

And from then on, Jesus' life was in danger. He would later have to suffer and lose his own life on a cross, but like Lazarus, he would also rise again from the tomb and continue to preach the word of God.

Final Words

Hey it's Ella Swan; I hope you enjoyed these enlightening Bible stories for kids. The only way for me to know what type of particular stories your child has enjoyed is by leaving an honest review on the product page, which will take less than 60 seconds of your time.

I will be able to create more tailored stories to your childs liking, and it will also help other parents discover this collection of amazing stories for kids!

Ella Swan :)

www.ingramcontent.com/pod-product-compliance
Lightning Source LLC
Chambersburg PA
CBHW021955170726
47994CB00021B/506